You, Me and the World We Inhabit

A Transactional Analyst's Perspective

©

By Eliott Green   Teaching & Supervising Transactional Analyst

Portrait of the Ponte Vecchio in Florence, Italy, showing the Vasari Corridor. Cosimo de' Medici had the corridor built to allow him and his family to move freely from one side of the city to the other, hidden from public scrutiny and those who might wish to harm them. It was a 'corridor of power', symbolising the divide between the people and the powerful. On May 9th 1938, Benito Mussolini walked with Adolf Hitler along the Vasari corridor.[1] Hidden from public view, both men admired the view of the River Arno from the Panoramic window at the centre of the bridge. Legend has it that the view so impressed the German Fuhrer, that he spared the bridge's destruction while other bridges in Florence were bombed. This deceptively beautiful bridge is symbolic of the world we live in, with the hidden elites occupying corridors of power while the rest of us remain naïve and blissfully ignorant of this parallel world.

---

[1] (Christopher Dobson, 2015)

First published in the United Kingdom 2021

Copyright © Eliott Green 2021

Eliott Green has asserted his right under the Copyright, Designs and Patents Act, 1998, to be identified as the Author of this work

All rights reserved. No parts of this publication may be reproduced or transmitted in any form or by any means, electronic or mechanical, including photocopying, recording, or any information storage or retrieval system, without prior permission in writing from the publishers

To contact the author for information or to leave feedback, please email:

Themindrevolutionfeedback@gmail.com

All client names and some descriptors have been changed to maintain confidentiality and anonymity

Introduction

There are few things more painful than a mind that has lost the plot. Sitting down in 2020 as the UK is in lockdown, the thought enters my mind: "Have we all gone mad?" Yet, if this is a collective madness, then the sane person is like the one-eyed man in the land of the blind. Or is he the pariah, the one who doesn't really belong, the one whose existence threatens all the others? If madness is defined as sticking out in a large crowd, then I guess the sane person is called 'mad'. However, if sanity is about being able to hold one's own thoughts, feelings and actions together under an umbrella of consistency and reason, then no, the person is not 'mad'.

I have used my 'lockdown' time to put down my thoughts in this short book. It includes a section entitled "About You: 'A Brief Guide to Transactional Analysis'" that serves to give you, the reader, a primer on Transactional Analysis. It is a system by which to examine your individual psychological make-up and personality. It aims to help you make better sense of yourself, to find your own voice. In so doing, it may help you understand others better too.

In Part Three, I reflect on what is going on around us in this world we all inhabit, how the way we think about ourselves and society is changing rapidly; how the concept of the 'individual' and that of 'individual freedom' is on the 'endangered species' list. I call this "The Mind Revolution". We are so driven by our desperate need to belong, to give up our history, to ignore the wisdom of our elders, to 'stay safe', 'stay alert', to conform to diktats that so many of us remain sceptical of, while others scream at us to put on our facemasks or take the knee. This once-proud society is at risk of breaking up and returning to medieval 'witch hunts' and mob violence. It is fast becoming deranged.

I have spent several years investigating this phenomenon and I do not believe we have arrived at this point organically; this is not a natural evolution of our society. Instead, it has been a socially and psychologically engineered phenomenon, an ideologically driven push to introduce a new metaphysics, to replace the Christian faith that has been dismantled in the secular West. It is one thing to remove a religion; it is quite another to replace it with something else. Yet this is what is being done, under the cover of naivety and by stealth.

Many of us are asleep as a revolutionary fervour seeks to destroy the successful West from within. We are passively allowing an imposed, oppressive ideology[2] to dictate our future. Christianity was far from perfect, yet its values kept the West together for 2,000 years. We need to rediscover

---

[2] (Trevor Phillips, 2020)

our confidence if we are to stand up against such tyranny and liberticide.

PART ONE

About Me

I was born and raised on a council estate in Gibraltar in 1958, at a time when the frontier was open between Gibraltar and Spain. I often visited relatives and friends in Spain and have fond memories of that period. Then, in 1967, a referendum was held so that the Gibraltarian people could decide their future either under the UK or Spanish sovereignty. The vote was overwhelmingly in favour of retaining British sovereignty (99.55%). However, in 1968, a small delegation of Gibraltarian lawyers and businessmen (the 'Doves' or 'Palomos'), held informal talks with the Spanish government in an attempt to establish a political settlement with Spain to solve the disputed status of Gibraltar. Once their letter was published in the Gibraltar Chronicle, it quickly led to disturbances as a large crowd formed in opposition to the motion. I witnessed scenes of violence and the destruction of property in an otherwise very peaceful city. I was only 9 at the time and still remember seeing many faces I recognised in the crowd and how full of hatred they were. They were no longer individuals, but a mass all acting as one organism, burning and menacing, overturning cars and a bus, breaking windows and chanting hateful threats against 'Los Palomos'. I remember thinking then what it would be like to be a

'Palomo', something akin to a 'Jew' in a pogrom; a pariah who had to be destroyed. To this day I am still wary of crowds and the groupthink that propels them to act in tandem. Reason would only restrain some, but other forces would instil rage, hatred and revenge resulting in mayhem and wanton destruction, completely oblivious to the effect of their action on innocent bystanders. This orgy of fanatical righteousness was being manipulated by a mischievous few, who knew how to create and maintain pandemonium and exerted malicious power over those who rioted.

This experience affected me deeply. Violence is something I abhor because it is about imposing someone's will on another. It forces a human being to do the bidding of another, akin to slavery. In the case of the crowd, forcing the individual to submit to the will of the collective. Even though I agreed with the result of the referendum and was on the side of the majority, I could not countenance the punishing of the minority. It was not justice. It had descended into mob rule. I decided on that fateful day in 1968, that I would work hard, get myself an education and leave Gibraltar. Ten years later, at the age of 19, I did precisely that. Heartbreaking though it was to leave behind friends and relatives as well as the city I loved, I was not prepared to live in a place where anyone's right to individual freedom of thought and speech was restricted by duress - the pressure to conform to the collective will.

I had a choice then, but in 2020, I fear that choice is similarly being restricted in the UK and elsewhere in the West. The unambiguous requirement to conform distinguishes the authoritarian regime from the libertarian one. That is, the group-will denies the individual his right to think differently. It is one thing to expect every individual to abide by democratically arrived at decisions. It is quite another to punish those who simply have a different attitude or who dare to be different. That was, after all, the push behind the Civil Rights movement that promoted equal rights for people of different races, colour, gender and sexual orientation. As a teacher and later a psychotherapist, I continue to believe in acceptance of these different characteristics and attitudes as traditionally formulated; I have long promoted the rights of all people and believe that we can all unify around a common humanity. I am not however in favour of forcing tolerance for modern reformulations based on politicised characteristics. This is too serious an issue to be turned into a childish playground game...a game called 'Righteousness' where the 'superior' punish those they regard as 'inferior'.

I qualified as a teacher of chemistry and biology in 1981. My first job was in Battersea, London, home to the riots in that same year. This was a 'deep end' introduction to the social issues that beset that community; it was this that motivated me to understand its impact on those I was teaching. I was particularly interested in the pastoral aspect of teaching and in understanding why many students struggled with the world of learning. Through the help of a mentor, I visited the homes of some students, spoke to their parents, and began to see why, for many, the home situation was not supportive of a calm and productive educational experience. Many parents were themselves struggling with their own lives, were unable to perform some of their parental duties, and required the children to look after them. Many of the children who exhibited poor behaviour and attendance at school were from homes where they were left to fend for themselves, had to look after a disabled parent, or whose parent struggled financially, sometimes as a result of an addiction. Most often, the child's world had been shattered by marital breakdown, and their being brought up by a sole parent or being put into foster care. There were many complex reasons as to why marriages had failed, and I remained compassionate, especially towards those that continued to try to bring stability to the lives of their children. However, for children, there was undoubtedly a price to pay. To compensate for the lack of a male role model, many boys in particular had joined gangs. Battersea, London was then considered a 'disadvantaged' community.

Lord Scarman wrote a report on the riots and concluded that "complex political, social and economic factors" created a "disposition towards violent protest."[3] The Scarman Report highlighted problems of racial disadvantage and inner-city decline, warning that "urgent action" was needed to prevent racial disadvantage from becoming an "endemic, ineradicable disease threatening the very survival of our society." It was evident that in the face of these social difficulties, education often took a backseat role. I learned that the child's lack of proper learning often was a symptom of a larger, wider issue; whilst Scarman focused on race and political/financial factors, I saw these as aggravating circumstances and not the cause of the rot. What I saw was a family breakdown issue that spilled out into the community and into the school.

The Family was no longer able to contain and nurture its children; it was increasingly failing to act as a stabilising entity by which to rear children. Regardless of the underlying origins behind this decline, that fact was evident. Be it caused by economics, race, anti-authority issues or other factors such as domestic abuse or infidelity, the family was no longer doing its job. This fact is often ignored in modern discussions of the social problems we face in 2020.

In 1984 I became Head of Chemistry at Red Hill School in Kent, a special residential school for 58 boys, aged 11-19, all of whom were extremely bright (IQs of 140-200), and who

---

[3] (Lord Scarman, 1981)

had Emotional and Behavioural Difficulties. Many had been expelled from numerous schools and their local authorities were at a loss to know what to do with them. Some had joined gangs and taken to a life of crime, while others were targeted by predatory paedophiles. Their families were not able to contain and nurture them, so they were sent away from home. Given how potentially bright these boys were, why were they 'unteachable' and so delinquent?

I was in for a massive shock and equally significant learning experience. The boys were pretty wild by comparison with the 'relatively compliant' Inner London kids I was used to. The school was described as a 'self-governing' school, which meant that the kids were in charge, not the adults. It was a very progressive environment, set up by Otto Shaw[4], a local magistrate, who had taken his ideas from A.S. Neill of Summerhill.[5] This structure did not ignore governance. Instead, it gave the children a stake in how governance was carried out. It was a more permissive environment than I was used to, more child-friendly, but it equally emphasised the role of personal responsibility. In essence, it did not practise licence, where kids could do whatever they wished. Instead, there were consequences to actions and inactions. There was a school court, presided over by three senior students. There, children sometimes appealed fines levied

---

[4] (Otto L Shaw, 1966)
[5] (Alexander Sutherland Neill, 1960)

by teachers and often presented well-argued defences. It is no surprise to learn that some of these children later went on to become successful barristers! Apart from the court at which attendance was compulsory, there was also a weekly Community Meeting where anyone could raise issues or put forward proposals on which everyone could vote. The teachers also attended these meetings, but their role was more as overseers rather than having direct involvement.

It was when I attended a Community Meeting for the first time that my interest was piqued. There I saw 11-year olds hold their own against much physically stronger 18-year olds. They were unafraid and could argue better than most adults I'd ever come across. They were unafraid to speak their truth, were passionate about their ideas and knew how to stand up for themselves. This was too good a learning opportunity to pass over, so I accepted the Head of Chemistry role.

I liked these kids from the outset, their feisty nature, their mischievousness, their humour and the gentle ribbing of me and one another. Some reminded me of my friends from the council estate, while others amused me with how socially clueless they were. What was striking was how different these kids were from one another, how independently-minded each was. Yet, they collectively bought into the Red Hill ethos and settled disagreements with the power of argument rather than with their fists.

What was life like for me as a teacher? It was an educational experience; a humbling one at times and exhilarating at others. For, whilst I sometimes saw poor behaviour, I saw this being dealt with by the boys themselves, sometimes via corrective punishment that was more onerous than I was used to in a state school. Sometimes kids were fined from their weekly pocket money, which they hated more than anything. They would then have to go around looking for paid work to make up the shortfall... only to discover that the tuck shop, on which they spent most of that money, was closed and they would have to wait several days before re-opening! Court punishments sometimes involved banning children from social events or requiring them to eat alone for a week. Sometimes they would have to act as 'Waker-upper', a much-detested role where they would be the one who woke up first and then had to wake up all the others – often to the predictable abuse coming from those still in the deepest slumber. Depending on the severity of the breach, the punishment was often specifically tailored to the individual and their historical patterns of misbehaviour. It certainly was not a one-size-fits-all punishment. It often was less of a punishment and more of a corrective action, designed to make the person more responsible and less selfish.

As a teacher, I soon learned that if I fined a student for bad behaviour, I'd better be prepared for the fine to be appealed in court. I could not assume that since I held a position of authority, I would likely be presumed in the right. Here it was the power of argument that was valued, not one's status. Little or no consideration was given to assertions or allegations that were devoid of evidence. The court environment did not indulge a 'victim mentality' and gave short shrift to anyone who had not constructed a proper charge or defence. It was not easy or straightforward to put forward a convincing argument for why I considered a behaviour as 'bad' for instance, since the counter-arguments were often ingenious and brilliant. Many did not subscribe to any faith and considered themselves atheists or amoral. Many lacked a sense of good and bad, a conscience. In the absence of a moral frame of reference, the Golden Rule "Don't do unto others what you wouldn't want done onto you" was the code being followed. These children used their skills to assert their point of view, their passion to appeal to the heart and their antisocial ability to manipulate and seduce an audience. Some later turned to politics as it ideally suited their sometimes-sociopathic tendencies.

What really struck me was the role of personal responsibility. Unlike what many outsiders thought, these kids were not living a life akin to 'Lord of the Flies'.[6] Nothing could be further from the truth. Instead, they were being trained in how to be personally responsible. They were

---

[6] (William Golding, 1954)

being taught how to take responsibility for their actions, rather than blame someone else. What better judges of the 'blaming technique' than those who used to be experts in blaming others?

So, while society was moving in the direction of absolving bad behaviour following Scarman, kids at this School were being held to account and learning the valuable lesson of taking personal responsibility. This is the difference between Freedom and Licence, between the educational theory of A S Neill [7] and the psychoanalytic theory of Erich Fromm.[8] For the former promoted human decency and a responsible "I-Thou" stance. The lesson to be learned was that in order to experience Freedom, one had to stop blaming others and take personal responsibility for one's plight. This Freedom had to be earned, yet was free and available to all. All one had to do was 'grow up' and become a responsible person.

Erich Fromm, on the other hand, sought to create a more permissive attitude and to remove external, moral restrictions from human interactions. His view resulted in the reformulation of moral regulators such as shame and guilt; by promoting 'Moral Relativism', he in effect removed moral conscience from human-to-human interactions. Lack of conscience led to an increase in Narcissistic individuals as

---
[7] (Jonathan Croall, 1983)
[8] (Erich Fromm, 1941)

well as sociopaths and psychopaths. It is indeed an irony then, that Erich Fromm wrote the foreword to A S Neill's book and spoke of the difference between liberty and licence. Whereas A S Neill promoted personal responsibility and mutuality as the route to real Freedom, Fromm believed in changing the role of the state and in the reformulation of morality itself, so that it no longer hindered the 'amoral' individual.

Almost from my first day at this most unusual school, I became a Counsellor to several of the boys. I began to slowly see the world through their eyes. To many of them, I held a position as the grand keeper of magic and alchemy - No matter how I might view myself as a twenty-five-year-old, slightly nervous, a Greenhorn and often wondering what I had let myself in for. I was struck by what they attributed to me, how they saw me. I learned that this was them projecting onto me, something I could do little about to shift. Instead of getting to know me slowly, I was tested by being put in difficult situations to see if I would over-react and leave. Many of these boys had experienced abandonment and had to test their relationship with me to breaking point, before they could afford to trust me. Even though I was new, naïve and still learning the ropes, this was a valuable insight into the personal and often imaginal lives of my students; it was their reality and a doorway into their magical way of thinking. It was as if they were lost in this parallel world, and preferred it to the distress they experienced in the grown-up world, and the world of their family back home; this fantasy world that simultaneously provided them with security and comfort, yet trapped them from achieving the potential of other boys of their age. Their 'locked-in' world was unusual then, but in 2020, we now see many people who are similarly trapped in a childlike world; a world of illusion, made-up rules and rituals, a 'Twilight Zone'. Otto Shaw had written a book called 'Prisons of the Mind'[9], the title of which captured their plight.

Boys at this school were each caught up in their fantasy worlds, stuck in battles with authority figures, 'tilting at windmills' as per Don Quixote.[10] Though cognitively very bright, they often presented as emotionally much younger than their chronological age would suggest. Boys would refer to "having a Wah", a term they used to describe someone having a meltdown. In such moments, an otherwise intelligent, reasonable, logical teenager would suddenly be taken over by a nihilistic temper tantrum, often resulting in them smashing objects in their path. 'Wahs' most often happened after court, when a fine was imposed or when they didn't win an appeal. Windows were often the target of their rage and some became experts in how to replace the glass they broke. That way, they didn't lose all their money on fines raised to pay for the damage!

---

[9] (Otto L Shaw, 1969)
[10] (Miguel de Cervantes Saavedra, 1605, 1615)

Trapped in their own 'Frozen time conglomerates',[11] the 'Wah' indicated that they had regressed emotionally to the age of a toddler. When their emotions took hold, the unresolved grievances from their childhood would periodically resurface. They would return to these immature angry displays when under stress. In such states, many of the boys were able to see the world only from their own point of view. They only saw 'the other' either as an obstacle to attaining their desires, or as a useful pawn. This is sometimes referred to as Narcissism, an egocentric or 'it's all about me' take on the world. This world then contrasted sharply with the real world outside, a world where reality was more objective, factual and evidence-based. It was not based on perception, but on how real people interacted with one another. My job was to help guide each person, both acknowledging their individual take while representing the take that others might hold. This helped them adjust to the demands that society would make of them when they left the school.

Little did I suspect then that, in the world of 2020, society would adopt many of the egocentric formulations it has, and that the immature schoolboy psyche would spread out and become prevalent in so many of us. Unfortunately, the

---

[11] (Barbara Ann Brennan, 1993)

independently-minded quality of the Red Hill boys did not similarly transfer itself into society.

Becoming both Head of Chemistry and a Counsellor was a steep learning curve. There was a lot for me to take in, to learn and adjust to. All the while I was surrounded by boys with a variety of brilliant minds, some of whom were extremely streetwise, others who had poor to non-existent social skills; it was a little daunting at first. I soon learned that whilst I was compassionate to their plight, I never forgot just how good many were in presenting themselves as the 'victim' of some injustice. My role was to acknowledge their feelings, but not to allow myself to get sucked into their world. Justice is something I passionately believe in, but it cannot be defined solely by one side.

Many were trapped in a world of suffering and immense pain. Their world view was often parochial, where they were raging against something they perceived as their enemy. A world of biased perception, rather than a world of discoverable truth. Their rage or hatred prevented them from working through their feelings and acted to block their life potential. They did not properly understand that others might view things differently, that there was learning to be had if only they allowed themselves to step outside of themselves and their fear. In terms made popular by Erik

Erikson,[12] they were stuck in a stage of personal development which he called 'Autonomy versus Shame & Doubt'. Here, the urge to exercise free choice and exhibit competence was opposed by the disabling effect of shame and lack of real confidence in one's competence. In this impasse, their frustration often manifested as rage and destruction. Blaming was used as a way of experiencing relief from the build-up of distress and anger caused by such personal stuckness. Only, this was just a temporary relief, since the person learned nothing by exporting their pain onto someone else.

My role was to remind them of the 'other', to encourage them to understand the bigger picture and not to let them get lost in a world of hurt and pain. The school provided a lot of training in psychoanalysis, psychology, psychotherapy, so I could always seek supervision should I struggle with some of the more complex issues. I sometimes got to meet the families of some of the students and once again, was able to view the larger world of those I counselled. Often it was the families that found it too difficult to parent these very gifted boys. Many boys would doubtlessly have fallen into a life of crime or become yet another statistic of the mental health system had this extraordinary school not existed. Instead, they often left with significant qualifications, including A levels. I was left

---

[12] (Erik Erikson, 1951)

with a sense of great satisfaction, in having helped turn round some of their lives and preparing them for the grown-up world they were about to enter. After 6 years, I left the school and began the next stage of my journey.

I started training as a Transactional Analysis Psychotherapist[13] in 1990. This approach allowed me to combine the observational, public world of the teacher (Functional model), with the private, hidden world of the psychotherapist (Structural model). It provided me with insight into the inner workings of my students. I was still teaching Chemistry and Biology to boys who had emotional and behavioural difficulties, then in the North of England. Most were very bright individuals with very high IQs, yet who functioned at levels of 80+. Why? I was intrigued by how emotion can eat into the intellect to such an extent as to prevent people from achieving their true potential... even resulting in many adopting criminal behaviours.

I realised that the boys were usually relying on their primitive instincts, feelings and imagination, rather than accessing their higher brain functions. They were capable of logic and reason, but preferred to default to the crude and undeveloped magical thinking, more prevalent amongst anti-socials and those of criminal mindset. Their anti-authority attitude made it a 'cool' and 'delinquent' way of

---

[13] (Ian Stewart & Vann Joines, 1987)

either belonging to gangs at home or of shunning the outside world and becoming isolated in their bedrooms; they had learned to 'dumb down' in order to belong back home. Many had to work through their emotional and psychological issues through counselling and psychotherapy. After some years of residing in school, this anti-authority attitude usually changed as they adjusted to the social norms of the school. Their way of belonging had changed and they often left well adjusted, to the norms of society.

In 1991, I became Head of Science at a therapeutic community. It accepted a wide range of children, of often low to moderate IQ, all of who were considered distressed and vulnerable. The community looked after children who had lacked adequate care in their families of origin and who needed both therapy and education. The Community believed in the restorative power of family, and was set up as a series of 'family units'; there was an emphasis on both containment and nurture, based on psychotherapeutic principles.[14] I used my knowledge of Transactional Analysis as well as my knowledge of science and education to help children receive an education; there were specialist therapists on-site who helped these children to recover from traumatic early years experiences.

---

[14] (Donald Winnicott, 1964)

Transactional Analysis enabled me to be aware of their world as well as my own. It helped me to stay out of the complex emotional dramas (Games) that these children were often embroiled in. I taught them the 'Drama Triangle' and the concept of 'Functional Ego States', which helped them understand why they often found playground time so distressing. They learned strategies for addressing disappointment via building resilience; space was made in the classroom to get them calm and ready for learning. I used the Functional Model to help them address their behaviour. I did not use the Structural Model, since there were therapists on-site whose job was to delve into their private 'inner' worlds. Nevertheless, the application of the TA Functional model often resulted in significant changes to their behaviour, especially their attitude to learning. For instance, they learned that they didn't have to behave badly just because one or two of their classmates were having a meltdown. This 'herd instinct' to join in with whoever was in distress was dealt with - the usual panic reaction had been for the whole class to follow the lead of the person in distress, by all running out of the classroom and causing mayhem. This stampede effect, caused by blind panic, was disruptive and put them at risk. Through the application of consistently clear, firm boundaries they allowed themselves to be 'psychologically held' and contained. Through class discussion to air grievances and distinguish real from imagined slights, they developed trust in others. Through the therapy, they each received, their original wounds were identified and healed. Through an ongoing partnership with their family groups, they received the nurture so often absent in the families of origin. As their erratic behavioural issues were addressed, their distress displays lessened and their energy became directed to the task of learning.

In 1992, I was approached by some GPs and offered the use of a consulting room. I set up an evening, part-time, private psychotherapy practice seeing adults, as individuals, couples and groups. I wrote 'A Brief Introduction to Transactional Analysis' - now updated, it forms the 'About You' part of this book. I aimed to summarise the theory of this personal, psychological world, developed by Dr Eric Berne [15] in the USA. Its scientific/medical approach puts the human being or person back into the centre of the study. By then, I applied Transactional Analysis theory to students who were considered slow learners and saw them develop learning strategies where there had been no learning discipline instilled in them. Many were subsequently able to sit and pass exams, something unthinkable before then. I then left teaching in 1994 to concentrate on my psychotherapeutic practice.

Throughout all my teaching and counselling, the Jungian concept of 'Individuation'[16] was central; that we each get to

---

[15] (Eric Berne, 1961)
[16] (Carl Jung, 1921)

know our own minds - how each of us thinks and feels - separate to the thoughts, opinions and beliefs of others. The process of individuation is one of achieving a sense of individuality, of who we really are, separate from the identities of others. By so doing we each begin to consciously exist as a full person in this world. This emphasis on self-discovery was central to my work as a psychotherapist, and it complemented my education as a scientist with its emphasis on the discovery of truth by applying logic and using facts to test hypotheses. Once people began to realise that they were able to think for themselves, it liberated them from having to believe what others believed. They became aware of the effects of external influences, such as their family, friends, culture, media, religion and education. It enabled them to make peace with their life history, grow in confidence and find a life purpose. It enabled them to engage in the process of 'growing up' and becoming a fully conscious, independent individual; an individuated person, able to define who they were and who they were not. In many cases it challenged their tribal loyalties, their attitudes, their friendships - in so doing, releasing themselves from the shackles of conformity.

I had worked with disturbed young people (i.e. Individuals who have psychological 'splits' in their personalities), and with their families since 1984, in my role as a Counsellor alongside my teaching duties. 'Splitting'[17] is a psychological defence that prevents individuals from individuating and becoming whole. Split individuals can only see things from one point of view. Everything for them is either black or white. They lack a nuanced or balanced stance on life. It is possible to work through this as long as the individual is supported by a group that is unified or integrated. Otherwise, it will persist if the supportive group is itself split. Splitting is the route to madness and can be found not only in individuals but in groups and organisations.

Before coming across Transactional Analysis I had acquired a Psychoanalytic understanding to help guide me in making sense of the 'human' psyche. Useful as this undoubtedly was, I yearned for a way of making sense that I could teach to others and get them to become experts in their own psyches. This fitted in with my philosophy that I acted as an enabling guide and not an expert Guru. I thought that each person would do best to discover who they were for themselves, rather than become indoctrinated by me. This has been a consistent theme of mine to this day!

From 1994, I worked as a therapist/counsellor for a large GP Practice alongside my growing private psychotherapy practice. Over the next 6 years in my NHS role, I developed and ran several therapy groups using TA principles. These

---

[17] (Thierry Bokanowski & Sergio Lewkowicz 2009)

groups became specialised in areas such as anxiety and depression, trauma, relationship difficulties, parenting issues, identity issues and food issues. The GP-funded role enabled me to work with a wide range of individuals who ordinarily could not access psychotherapy. I was also able to provide a service to other GP practices who would refer individuals to my groups.

In 1996, I qualified as a Certified Transactional Analyst (clinical). By then I had a full-time, private psychotherapy practice and started running educational workshops in TA for those in therapy as well as their family, friends and members of the public. I aimed to create an open educational community, which encouraged scepticism, debate and discussion. I ran numerous courses in Introductory TA as well as Intermediary and Advanced seminars. By 2003 I had become a Teaching & Supervising Transactional Analyst (Psychotherapy). This meant that I trained others in how to become Transactional Analysis Psychotherapists.

In 2001, I took on a part-time, voluntary role as Chair of Professional Practice for the Institute of Transactional Analysis, an organisation numbering approximately 1,500 individuals. I enjoyed being a part of the organisation and being able to give something back to the TA community. In 2004 I became its Chief Executive Officer for a period of two years. I knew that the organisation was facing challenging times and that many would resist the changes that were necessary for it to remain relevant. The ITA was originally formed as a small, voluntary and friendly association, but had grown into a large, business-like and professional body. The task was to update its structure and modernise its outlook, without it splitting into different camps. The organisation as a whole struggled to accept the necessary changes, achieve autonomy and adjust to its new role. I was aware that there were many vested interests, agendas and factions that would not hold together for too long. Having achieved my goals, I left my role in 2006. The inevitable 'split' happened a few years after I left, with some senior members leaving and a new body representing UK Transactional Analysis being formed.

In my psychotherapy practice, I worked extensively with individuals, but I developed a liking for group work. This different way of working brought individuals into contact with the social pressure of the collective. Group work counteracted the often-isolating effect of individual therapy. In the group arena, everyone was encouraged to take an active part and to find their own voice. Rules were agreed at the start, as was a code of conduct in how to receive and give feedback. One such rule adopted by my groups was to not engage in 'Naming, Shaming or Blaming' since these are simply ways of avoiding personal responsibility. Instead, they learned how to receive and give constructive, honest feedback and to become aware of their own bigotry. Transactional Analysis was originally developed as a group psychotherapy and provided a theoretical basis for making sense of interactions in a group. Individuals learned how their behaviour impacted others, the games they played and how to break out of them. By hearing how they impacted others, individuals were encouraged to look more deeply into their psyches through introspection. Thus, groups enabled people to develop better social skills, feel more confident and indulge less in nursing their hurt feelings. They were encouraged to explore and let go of their hidden grievances and to become powerful grownups. It was remarkable how the collective stance of the group often served to both acknowledge and mollify the distressed stance of an individual; the alchemy[18] present when the collective and the individual stances worked together, often producing extraordinary results. Group work can be a very powerful therapeutic tool, in many ways more powerful than individual therapy.

I started my first therapy group in 1992 and for the first twenty years, I saw numerous individuals benefiting from the experience. I saw many become individuated and find their own voice. Many let go of extremist positions once they were faced with their impact on those they trusted and

---

[18] (Barbara Somers, 2004)

the relationships they forged. During that time period, I ran six long term and over twelve short term groups.

However, I began to question the benefits of group work from 2010 onwards. I started to notice an attitude of intransigence and belligerence take hold amongst several group members, where many were willing to sacrifice friendships and relationships on the altar of righteousness. People in groups began to fall out as identity politics entered the arena. PC culture conflicted with the process of individuation since it introduced an artificial, exogenous expectation to the mix. Individuation was being restricted by new 'moral' codes that curtailed freedoms of speech, expression and individuality; a new form of 'moral' pressure was being applied to people who were trying to release themselves from the old moral shackles of societal programming. Imposed Collectivisation, or being required to obey arbitrary and often spurious social diktats, is precisely what therapy had sought to resist.[19] Its effect was to severely restrict introspection and maintain people in an unindividuated or regressed state.

With the proliferation of smartphones and social media, more people were getting their 'belonging needs' met from niche groups, instead of from the therapy group. The need to 'belong' to their social groups exacted a high price. It

---

[19] (Paul Vitz, 1977)

pitted the liberty of the individual to think their own thoughts with the conformity demanded by belonging to their social groups. In the therapy groups, this led to an increase in 'splitting', a hardening in attitudes and an unwillingness to find common ground through reason. In short, an increase in bigotry that refused to lend itself to introspection. I experienced the same 'splitting' phenomenon when I worked as a consultant to organisations. My therapeutic colleagues reported similar experiences and most had already closed their therapy groups.

Although 'splitting' is an area I have specialised in, I had always relied on a cohesive society as a backdrop or backup. I relied on a society and groups where people disagreed, but found common ground. Instead, Freud's 'Narcissism of Small Differences'[20] was taking hold; people were falling out because of the small differences, despite agreeing on the vast majority of issues. In the end, many people were unwilling to realise that their stance might be an extreme one and one that would take them out of the balanced group consensus and of the centre-ground. In society itself, the notion of 'common sense' was becoming both less common and making less sense. In the words of William Butler Yeats in his poem, 'The Second Coming', "Things fall

---

[20] (Sigmund Freud, 1930)

apart; the centre cannot hold."[21] This reflected the changing nature of society at large, where extremist positions were being regarded as 'normal'; what was less evident in 2010 is so apparent now in 2020 - a society that is so obviously split. Having persevered with ever more challenging, intense splitting, my concerns grew. I concluded that the groups had become anti-therapeutic and potentially a source of harm rather than good. Reluctantly, I decided to close my remaining therapy groups in 2018.

I reflected on the assault on Individuation by its arch-rival – Collectivisation. That psychotherapy was becoming less about enabling people to discover their own minds and more about enabling people to fit in better into society. The term 'Mental Health' was being used as a way of herding people into what society deemed right. This meant that the free-thinking individual was expected to conform to the collective will. That instead of challenging all bigotry and dogma, psychotherapy itself was becoming a movement that promoted a new form of bigotry and dogma. In essence, the very opposite of therapy was being sold as 'therapy'. Therapy was becoming more of a surrendering of individual consciousness than a journey of discovering our full potential as individuals.

---

[21] (William Butler Yeats, 1920)

In order to make sense of what was happening in society, I set about reading, meeting with colleagues and meditating. I became an ADRg accredited Family Mediator in 2011, and in 2012 I was awarded a degree in Law. I was simultaneously pursuing my interest in Transpersonal or Psychospiritual domains, writing and teaching about matters to do with the Soul and Spirit in Human Nature[22]. I learned about Philosophy and Politics alongside History, World Affairs and Conflict Resolution. All this learning enabled me to write Part Three of this book. So, there you have it, a brief summary of my professional journey. Having worked in the field of helping others for close to forty years, what have I learned?

People are both simple and complex. Transactional Analysis is a great tool to help you start making sense of who you are. It is a theory of the personality, of what goes on inside of us as well as between us; yet there is more to being a person than that. Each of us has an origin story and therefore a history and culture from which we've emerged. We come from a family, however constituted, and have all experienced some level of care and nurture to get us to this point. Undoubtedly - for some of us - that care was compromised, as I saw first-hand when I visited the homes of some of my students. Often this inadequate care continued throughout several generations. It was

---

[22] (Thomas Moore, 1992)

heartbreaking to watch people blame one another for their failings, instead of developing the self-discipline required to get themselves out of a hole. Yet, many make it regardless.

There is a spirit in all of us that can transcend the hand we've been dealt. When we connect with this aspect of ourselves, we can build a better future for ourselves and our children. We can be proud that we've improved the world in some small way, by our toil, by spreading a little hope and happiness. This is why the family is so important. It is our place of arrival after birth, our first nursery, playground, frame of reference. It imprints our sense of belonging, a longing for love and connection, for being a part of something bigger, something we can call home. Yet, some of us have experienced families full of inadequate care, where those who are tasked with caring for us have failed in that duty. Do we in turn blame our parents and upbringing for our failings? Do we give up or can we acknowledge the past and move beyond it? That is the purpose behind this book. Looking on at the state of this world in 2020, it is easy to lose hope in humankind... yet that is because there are so many grievance merchants that peddle a message of 'unfairness', and not enough elders to counteract them.

People like Otto Shaw saw bright young children embark on a life of crime, yet cared enough to set up a new school to educate them. This was not an easy undertaking, but a necessary one. It was his pioneering spirit that made a difference to the lives of those forgotten children. Hope for the future does not lie in blaming others, or the past. It involves digging deep into the core of who each of us is and believing in our shared future. It is not in grievance that we will find ourselves, nor in dividing ourselves as people into ridiculous identity boxes. For the blame game is what dysfunctional families get caught up in. We need to give up on blaming others for our own weaknesses and develop the will to resist those that wish to destroy our society and way of living. Personal responsibility shows us the way.

The book that follows is divided into two further parts. Part Two is the theory that will help you make sense of yourself and others. Transactional Analysis is a theory that emerged during the time of the Civil Rights movement in the 1960s. It is a powerful theory because it reminds us of the essence of human nature.

Most significantly, it is a theory that believes in the concept of 'growing up'. What is this?

We often use the phrase 'grow up', and many hear it as a pejorative. That is, expressing contempt or disapproval of one's attitude or behaviour. Whereas that may be true in some instances, it limits the full meaning behind the words.

Growing up is an essential part of the human condition. We grow up physically as our bodies mature developmentally from that of a child to that of an adult. Just as our physiology and anatomy change, other changes need to keep up with each of us becoming a grown-up. Cognitive changes need to take place, developing our magical ways of thinking into ones that use logic and reason as well. Our behaviours need to change so that we learn to settle disputes with dialogue rather than rely on violence or threats to the person. Our emotions need to develop from egocentric ones to ones that see others as living people, each with their own thoughts, feelings and dreams, often very different from our own.

Growing up is an act of individuation; one that allows each of us to realise our full potential. It means developing a fully mature way of thinking and feeling - of relating to a wide range of ideas and knowledge - we must not allow ourselves to be defined and restricted by the lapses in care and inherent inequalities we have encountered. Instead of relying on the blame narrative, we must not allow ourselves to be trapped by staying needy and dependent, therein remaining emotionally immature.

So, what then is 'growing up'?[23] I believe it is about us individually, taking personal responsibility for our attitudes,

---

[23] (Jean Illsley Clarke & Connie Dawson, 1989)

thoughts, feelings and behaviours. It is not about obediently following an external or 'group code'. To grow up we must develop our own 'internalised' responsibility for ourselves and others; growing up presents a challenge to the young, narcissistic part within us all. Fundamentally, it is about treating oneself as a fully sentient person as well as treating all others with equal consideration. A true 'I – Thou' stance. It is about seeing oneself as a subject, not an object. A subject is alive, with feelings, ideas, desires, dreams, fears, doubts and courage. An object has none of the above. In addition to that, it is about waking up to the fact that everyone is a subject and no one is an object – no matter how objectionable we might find another!

To grow up is to appreciate all life, especially the potential in all persons. Instead of engaging in victimhood mentality and its divisive ideology, it is about raising the human being above the poor containment and nurture offered by the dysfunctional family and modern educational system. To grow up means to learn to become the elders of tomorrow, instead of tearing down the elders of the past. Evolution builds upon what has come before it. It does not tear down that which it finds difficult or restrictive. For that is the domain of revolution, the setting fire to everything because it could not be bothered to keep what works and work to change that which can be improved.

To grow up means becoming a reformist rather than a revolutionary person. The reformist appreciates what is good while remaining sceptical of what he sees as bad. He wants to improve things while remaining committed to the whole. In contrast, the revolutionary has given in to his nihilistic impulse and become cynical. The cynic does not distinguish between the good and the bad. He has given up and sees nothing of value. Conversely, the 'grown-up' keeps the baby and throws out the bathwater!

Part Three of this book looks at the world we now inhabit. It is a society that is in turmoil, one that is psychologically 'split' into irreconcilable parts. I aim to show that this is not a natural state of affairs. Instead, it has been socially engineered and is funded by those that do not subscribe to the values that underpin the West. Groups of people have been psychologically manipulated to turn on other groups. Grievances have been deliberately stoked, so as to turn people against people. A new religious war is upon us and I aim to wake people up to this reality. The Blame Game developed in dysfunctional families has spread outwards into communities and now into society at large. Lord Scarman was right on that score. However, whereas he pointed to race and political/financial factors, I still believe it is family breakdown that is at its core.

I have been intimately involved with families all my life. On the council estate, there was an open-door policy, so I would wander into different homes and appreciate the various families in action. It was my first training ground. I followed that up when I qualified as a teacher and once again as a counsellor. I saw healthy relationships and why they worked as well as unhealthy ones and why they failed. Such first-hand experience, coupled with training in Family and Systemic Therapy, led me to make important realisations. I concluded that there were two vital ingredients to successful relationships and functional families. The first was Love or Care. When people cared about each other and were willing to put the other person's needs first at times, there was a loving bond that could withstand many trials that life threw at them. In contrast, infidelity was a sign that the loving bond had been broken. The second ingredient was Justice or Fairness. That is a means of resolving conflict without resorting to violence or threats against the person. Shouting, swearing, breaking objects, blaming and name-calling all figured but did not necessarily lead to family breakdown. What did often break the fairness bond was domestic abuse, especially emotional violence, such as abject cruelty and physical or sexual abuse. Often the man would leave and the woman was left to bring up the children on her own and in poverty.

Such abandonment is what I encountered in many of the children I counselled. Whereas some parents ensured that their children were adequately cared for after the divorce, not all showed that consideration. All too often the children's lives were shattered by parents who were too wrapped up in their own world to realise the damage done to their children.

What tears a family apart are its differences and how these are held. In a functional family, there are differences, but these are not allowed to grow and take over from all the other delicate connections that bind us. There need to be ways of resolving conflict and differences and a will to do so. Otherwise, the grievances will reach a point where a 'split' is reached and alienation becomes evident. **Resentment can overpower love**. The prevention of such fallings-out was once the province of family elders, those who were considered wise and experienced. I remember the respect that teachers used to be accorded as well as doctors, lawyers, clergy, journalists, politicians... All of that is now in our past. In our 'engineered' society, the elders have been exposed, ridiculed and allowed themselves to be silenced. This is not a natural development, but one forced by political and psychological means.

When Dr Martin Luther King Junior[24] spoke his famous words on Racism, he believed in a world where each person would not be judged by the colour of their skin, but by the content of their character. That is, we are judged by what

---

[24] (Dr Martin Luther King Jr, 1991)

we make of our lives, by the values we live by and not by immutable factors such as race. You may not like me or I may not like you, but we both have a right to exist, to live our own lives and to hold different views. This definition was one that decent people all over the world resonated with.

In 2020, the more extreme Malcolm X[25] definition has seen a comeback. It seeks to divide people according to their skin colour and promotes an ideology based on segregation. It is based on a belief that racism is institutionalised and systemic; that white people have designed the world to oppress blacks and other minority groups. Thus, Critical Race Theory[26] introduces a belief system that goes much further than Lord Scarman did in 1981; it ignores other factors, such as nuclear family disintegration, which contributes to a sense of injustice felt by many. By blaming all injustices on skin colour, it stokes grievances and pits person against person so creating disunity. A righteous ideology is being pumped out into our culture; an ideology that justifies violence in its name. Such extreme politics and ideologies appeal to the immature mind rather than to a more-experienced and wise psyche.

---

[25] (Malcolm X & Alex Haley, 1987)
[26] (Richard Delgado et al, 2017)

I have always viewed 'splits' as arising from competing fears within an individual. One fear usually ends up being seen as imaginary or less important than the other. How a person comes to that realisation best comes from individuation and finding one's voice. Through the freedom to voice their own concerns as well as becoming aware of external societal expectations, the individual is encouraged to find the balance that is right for him. It is important in therapy, to allow the space for that to happen and to avoid interfering with that process through indoctrination. In our current society, however, there is enormous pressure on the individual to give up on their voice and to follow the herd. Modern therapy has begun to resemble the traditional indoctrination, it so sought to resist and separate itself from. In my opinion, it has become 'religious' in its inherent bias or singular worldview.

Our world is in danger of tearing itself apart, in the same way as I experienced in so many families, my organisational work and my therapy groups. Splitting threatens harmonious relations because it is divisive in its nature. It happens when we forget that which unites us and instead seek to destroy the cohesiveness that holds us together. It is the opposite of healing and serves only to promote madness and chaos. We choose such a path at our peril.

PART TWO

About You: A Brief Introduction to Transactional Analysis

Transactional analysis is a model for understanding human behaviour and psyche, developed by the late Dr Eric Berne, in the 1950s and 60s. It was originally developed as a means of addressing what goes on between people, be they couples, groups, families or organisations. Transactions are the interactions that occur when we signal or communicate with each other. The analysis of transactions enables the Transactional Analyst to identify games and develop new, healthier strategies to replace old, unhealthy and familiar patterns of behaviour.

As well as external communication between people, Transactional Analysis considers the internal communication that takes place within each of us. This communication is most often taking place unconsciously, or outside of our awareness. Transactional Analysis is, therefore, able to address both the private psyche of the individual (via psychotherapy) and the public communication between people (via behavioural therapy).

This ability to address both inner (intrapsychic) and outer (interpsychic) world experiences serves to distinguish Transactional Analysis from other forms of psychotherapy. It is based on what is happening to the client in the present, as a means of showing him where and how he is trapped in hurtful or destructive patterns that affect his everyday life. TA as it is called for short is based on three philosophical principles:

People are OK. We all have worth, value and dignity as people. There are no 'better' or 'worse' people as a result of the characteristics we are born with e.g. Race, gender, etc. People may make different choices and we may disagree about these. These constitute the 'content of our characters'. At times I may not like nor accept what you DO, but always I accept who you ARE. I may not like you or you like me, but we both have a right to our views, to think differently, to non-violently express our points of view and to exist on this planet.

Everyone has the capacity to think for themselves - except for the severely brain-damaged. We cannot be MADE to feel or behave in particular ways by others, or by our surroundings. 'We are responsible for our own feelings and behaviour.' However, under duress or in a trance state, we can be induced to take on another person's will. Likewise, we can think very differently if we are afraid, or have adapted to the norms of a group or a cult. Real thinking involves being individuated as an individual and not being the mouthpiece of an advantageous position, ideology or religion.

People decide to be the way they are. This applies to the non-biological, 'character-determined' aspects of the human condition. We are responsible for the decisions we make - to make the best of our lives. It is about taking personal responsibility for the decisions we make, rather than resorting to blaming others for the poor choices we may have made. Instead, it is about tracing the decisions and changing them for new and more appropriate decisions. 'These decisions can be changed,' through an application of personal agency.

TA is a contractual form of intervention. It has clear goals and direction. The contract is agreed upon between the client and Transactional Analyst at the start of their work together. This specifies clearly what outcome the client intends from the interaction, be it a change in attitude, feeling, response or action. The responsibility for change rests with the client who is expected to take the initiative in his own reflections. TA uses simple language to get across the complex theory. The client is encouraged to explore TA ideas and to become aware of how they might apply to him. Part of the work will involve learning about self and others, and becoming aware of how we all go about unconsciously setting up problems for ourselves. To be effective, TA demands personal agency i.e. Active involvement and sustained commitment. Those seeking help from it must be prepared to be confronted by their own self-destructive behaviour.

TA is a Humanistic psychotherapy (Moreno, Maslow, Rogers) and is distinct from Psychoanalytic (Freud, Jung, Erikson) and Behavioural (Pavlov, Skinner) approaches. TA does have some links with the other two camps, but several key ideas set it apart.

The Structural Ego-state model

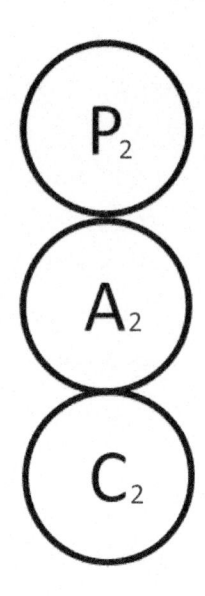

P_2

A_2

C_2

An ego-state is a set of related thoughts, feelings and experiences or states of mind. Each person has three distinct ego states and therefore three different ways of being himself. The number 2s indicate that these are the fully-developed, mature version of each ego state.

Sometimes I may think, feel and experience myself in ways that I have copied and internalised from others around me, such as my family and teachers who were parent figures for me. This is where I store real people and their different psyches. When I do so, I am in my PARENT (P2) ego-state.

When I think, feel and experience myself in response to what is going on around me, here-and-now, using all the resources available to me as a grown-up person, I am in my ADULT (A2) ego-state.

At times I may return to childhood ways of thinking and feeling, and experience myself as I did when I was a child. This is where I store my own experiences, feelings, thoughts and imaginings. Then I am in my CHILD (C2) ego-state.

The Structural model is the one used by psychotherapists in addressing issues to do with the private psyche of individuals. Knowing which ego-state we are in at any particular point is an important part of TA psychotherapy. Each ego-state contains its own information on values, feelings and ways of being. Because the experience in any one ego-state is often significantly different to that in the others, a person's beliefs, feelings and state of mind may be very different depending on which ego state is in charge at any particular time. The person may then experience internal conflict as he shifts out of one ego-state and into another. Confusion, depression, inappropriate anger, overwhelming sadness and addiction are some of the ways in which he may express his inner conflict. As he finds out the felt content of each ego-state, he starts to separate out the different parts of himself, enabling the resolution of that conflict to take place.

For instance, Julie may have high expectations of success in her Parent, resulting in her being a very driven person. However, she may have low self-esteem in her Child. This results in her not really believing in herself, doubting she has what it takes to be successful. This combination sometimes overwhelms her Adult and causes her distress whenever she is under pressure over deadlines. Were Julie to present in therapy, she would be encouraged to explore both the source of her high expectation in P_2 and the origin of her low self-esteem in C_2. She would learn to recognise which ego state was in charge at any given point, enabling her to make new choices in A_2. She might decide to address the compulsive nature of her high expectations and take steps to build up her self-esteem, to learn to value and like herself as a person. Her A_2 would no longer get overwhelmed by the other two ego states.

When a client comes to therapy, they are usually distressed and not as composed as they ordinarily would be. Nevertheless, they are still in their persona, the face they want to show to the world. To get to what is really going on, the Transactional Analyst looks deeper. He makes use of behavioural indicators such as tone of voice, the words used by the person, his gestures and body posture. By paying close attention to these behavioural indicators, the TA therapist builds up a picture of how that person gets caught up in predictable patterns such as the games they play. Likewise, in a therapy group, how they interact with others and how their unique history influences them or plays a part in their present. At times, a person will regress and re-experience themselves as they were as a child, or even replay one of their parents or caregivers. Behaviours alone are not enough, however, to successfully diagnose which structural ego state a person is in. Behaviours serve to point the way, as long as they are backed up by Phenomenological, Social and Historical evidence. Behaviours then are clues to aid in ego state diagnosis. However, they need to be used with caution.

For instance, "You're in your Parent" said to someone who shakes his index finger is simply not universally true (James, 1974). "The pointed index finger may be a Parental admonition, an Adult indicator, or a Child's accusation" (Berne 1966). Behaviours are not ego states, even though we often describe behaviours as 'parental', 'childish' or 'adult'. In TA we use a behavioural model, called the FUNCTIONAL MODEL, to separate out behaviours that may then, in turn, be used to help diagnose ego states. Confusingly perhaps, these behavioural states are called Functional Ego States:

The Functional Model:

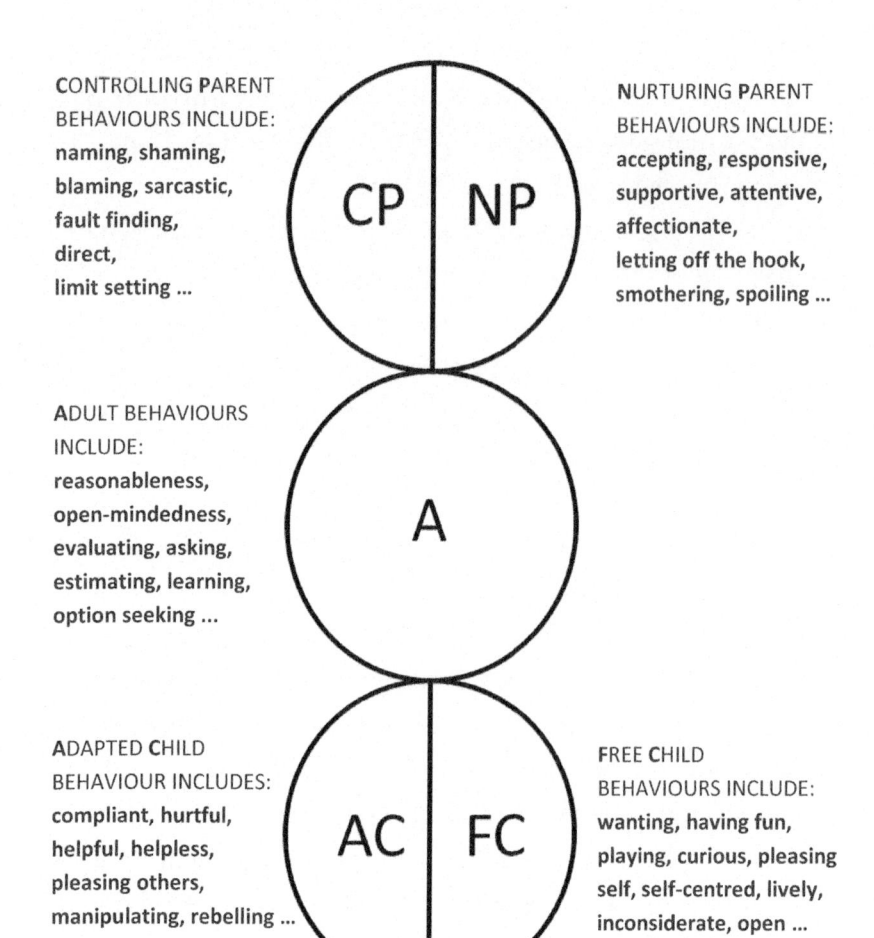

CONTROLLING PARENT BEHAVIOURS INCLUDE:
naming, shaming, blaming, sarcastic, fault finding, direct, limit setting ...

CP

NP

NURTURING PARENT BEHAVIOURS INCLUDE:
accepting, responsive, supportive, attentive, affectionate, letting off the hook, smothering, spoiling ...

ADULT BEHAVIOURS INCLUDE:
reasonableness, open-mindedness, evaluating, asking, estimating, learning, option seeking ...

A

ADAPTED CHILD BEHAVIOUR INCLUDES:
compliant, hurtful, helpful, helpless, pleasing others, manipulating, rebelling ...

AC

FC

FREE CHILD BEHAVIOURS INCLUDE:
wanting, having fun, playing, curious, pleasing self, self-centred, lively, inconsiderate, open ...

There are 5 recognised 'behaviour states' or Functional ego states. Unlike the 'structural ego states', which are hidden and private, functional ego states are observable and public. They are like the gears in a car, each with its own unique characteristics. They describe the person's outward behaviour, not their inner motivation.

Each Functional ego state can have positive and negative aspects. Since they are observable, they are useful to the behavioural transactional analyst, serving to help change behaviour.

Behaviours are the outward manifestation of a person's private psyche. They reveal a part of what is going on internally, but not necessarily the whole picture. For instance, a person may choose to go along with whatever is going on in the group they belong to, but privately may have unvoiced reservations. They are ambivalent. Judging the behaviour alone is to miss their disquiet.

For instance, David may have views on women that are not shared by the group he is part of. He might keep his opinions to himself for fear of attracting their wrath. The group might be misogynistic yet he might feel well disposed towards women. Or, it could be the other way round, with him being the misogynist.

The Functional model is a way of addressing the behaviours that David wishes to change. This may or may not resolve the underlying issues. For instance, David may wish to develop the courage to speak up for his views. He wishes to become more assertive as he no longer wants to appease others. Or, he may wish to find another group that better represents his views. These are behavioural outcomes.

The TA behavioural therapist will need to look at how much time and energy David uses in each of his 5 Functional Ego States. This will give a baseline picture called an 'Egogram'. Together David and the therapist will need to decide on what the desired outcome will look like in terms of the new egogram. He may need to develop the CP and AC or the NP and FC. He may need to develop options in A. In agreeing on a contract, both client and therapist need to be realistic, lawful and mindful of what likely consequences will follow the behavioural changes being planned.

David may develop a more assertive stance, yet his friends may shun him for it. Or, he may decide to find a group that better matches his private views. This will mean letting go of former friends and making new ones. In other words, behavioural changes will often lead to other changes, often social, work or even personal ones.

Should David wish to look deeper into making changes to his attitudes, he would need to look at the Structural model and engage a TA psychotherapist. Attitudes, beliefs and feelings underpin behaviours but are not necessarily addressed through behavioural change alone. Should David realise that he is a misogynist and choose to change his misogynistic stance, he would not simply choose to look for a group of non-misogynists. He would also need to delve deeper into his psyche and address his underlying feelings, belief system and how he has arrived at being misogynistic. He might learn that there are other forms of sexual prejudice and people bias, such as misandry and misanthropy. Biases can underpin our attitudes and warp our stance on life and in relationships. David is unlikely to get to this by only looking at his behaviour.

With a TA psychotherapist, he would explore the origins of his attitudes. They might reside in his P_2 as a prejudice passed down to him, or he might have decided on it through his own experiences in C_2. He can then choose to update the belief and replace the old with new decisions in A_2.

We each inhabit two worlds. The external world we share is the world of DOING, best described by the Public Functional model. The other world is the personal private world of BEING, best described by the Private Structural model.

The Structural/Functional Interface:

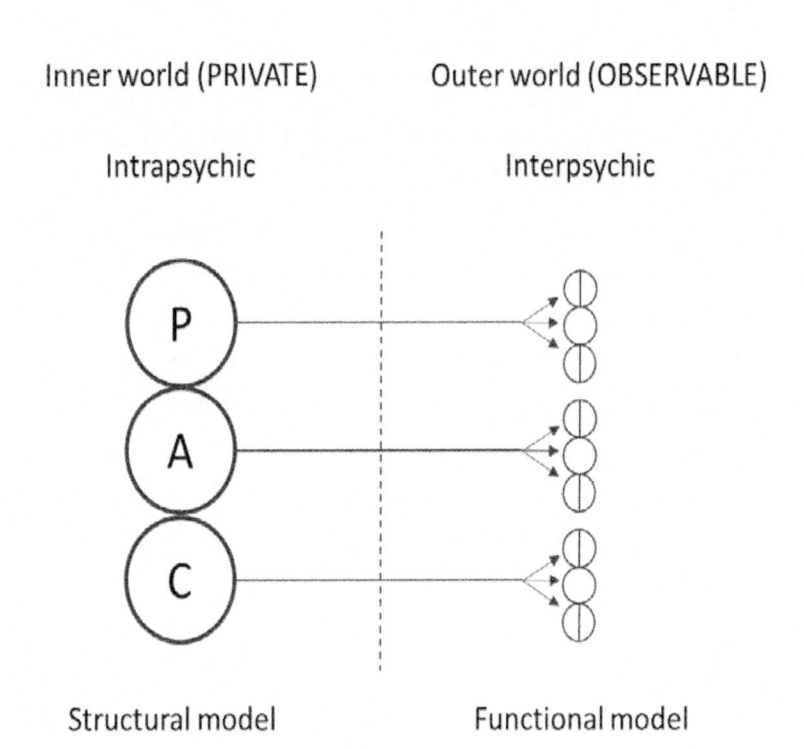

Inner world (PRIVATE)   Outer world (OBSERVABLE)

Intrapsychic   Interpsychic

Structural model   Functional model

Developed from Mary Cox TSTA

Just how do the PRIVATE (structural) and PUBLIC (functional) models interrelate? The interface between these two worlds was arguably Berne's greatest achievement – however, it was also the area of TA that attracted the most criticism. It resulted in people applying TA theory incorrectly and confusing intrapsychic (hidden) with interpsychic (observable) processes and vice versa. It was not the theory that was at fault, but its over-popularisation and subsequent misunderstanding. The following explanation aims to put this right.

The observable or behavioural functional ego states are like gears in a car, which can be chosen. Hence a person can act in any of 5 ways as described previously. i.e. CP, NP, A, AC or FC. The Adult in the functional model is defined very differently from the Adult Structural Ego State. That is because a person can appear to function in a reasonable, open-minded and option-seeking manner (functional Adult). However, that does not necessarily mean that they are coming from their here-and-now, Adult ego state (structural Adult). They could have chosen the Adult (functional) gear from their Parent or Child (structural) ego state. They may give the appearance of Adult but this is not necessarily so.

Is this important? Yes. If the person is not actually in Adult (structural) they may not be stable under stress. Their mask will start to crack. That then is the realm of psychotherapy. The psychotherapist needs to know which structural ego state a person is in at any given time. To do this, the therapist needs to use information that is more than simply the way a person behaves, or the functional model. By taking a detailed history, the therapist gets information that helps with that diagnosis. How did they behave in the past and what historical patterns of behaviour might be influencing the present? Additionally, by observing the client's social interactions, they get a sense of how that person interacts with others, engages in games, what sort of games etc. Lastly, the therapist looks for phenomenological evidence. That is, moments when the client momentarily regresses to developmentally - younger experiences (indicates Child) or uses responses that appear 'as if their training has kicked in' (indicates Parent). Having established where a person is coming from, the process of helping them change the internal dance can begin – the process of growing up, so that the Adult (structural) takes charge of the other two ego states.

John came into therapy with 'anger issues'. He would be a kind and thoughtful partner to his girlfriend most of the time. However, he would sometimes fly off into a rage, often unpredictably, and cause distress to her. When he calmed down, he would regret his outbursts, but feared she might leave him if he couldn't find a way out of this pattern.

John learned that his mum and dad had a similar relationship and that his father had left home when he was very young. John's anger issues had started shortly after the birth of his own son. Before that, he described the relationship with his girlfriend as fun and convivial.

Functionally, John's behaviours indicated that publicly he was in a fight between his Controlling Parent and his Rebellious (Adapted) Child. He showed little Nurturing Parent, functional Adult or Free Child energy. When he entered Adapted Child, he became red-faced and raging, as if he were a toddler throwing his toys out of a pram. The question then was: what was going on in his private world? In getting to know him, I assessed that **Structurally**, he was almost exclusively in his Child ego state C_2. He had no P_2 energy to intervene, and his A_2 would become overwhelmed. This meant that his Child ego state C_2 was excluding the other two and that he would need to be both confronted and nurtured.

In a therapy group, he experienced others who would intervene from their A_2 and P_2 whenever he began to appear agitated, a sign that his rage was building up. Through a mixture of firm boundaries and kind nurture on the group's part, he learned how to control his temper. He eventually realised that he was jealous of the love that his son was getting from his partner. His outbursts were unconsciously designed to test just how much his partner loved John, but also whether he might repeat what his own dad had done to him by leaving home. These and other realisations helped John come to terms with his conflicted C_2 and balance this with a stronger P_2 and calmer A_2.

Communication Model - Transactions, Strokes, Time Structuring:

Transactions:

When I communicate with you, I can choose to address you from any one of my five functional ego states. You can reply in turn from any one of your functional ego states. This exchange of information is called a Transaction. Transactions can be COMPLEMENTARY, where the ego state addressed is the one that responds to the original source – a 'boomerang effect'. Such transactions can carry on indefinitely. Complementary transactions are the most efficient way of exchanging information. Socially, however, they can become boring.

EXAMPLE of a Complementary Transaction

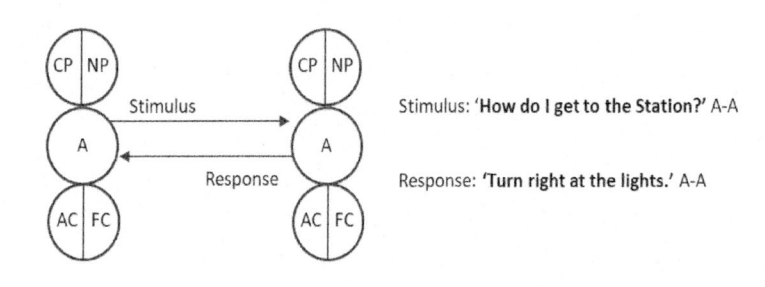

Stimulus: **'How do I get to the Station?'** A-A

Response: **'Turn right at the lights.'** A-A

Transactions can be CROSSED, where the ego state addressed is not the one that responds – or responds to an ego state different from the one that started the proceedings. Such transactions usually result in a break in communication by denying the 'boomerang effect'. This indicates that either one person has deliberately attempted to interrupt proceedings or, most often, that something else is going on – a type of spell or transference. Left unaddressed, this could be an indication that a game is afoot. A misunderstanding, perhaps, leading to hurt feelings maybe? Comedy relies on crossing transactions, as does creativity, in producing the unexpected.

EXAMPLE of a Crossed Transaction

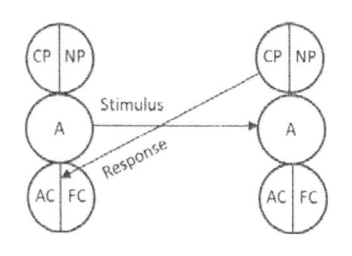

Stimulus: 'What time is it?' A-A

Response: 'Time you learned to say please.' CP-AC

Sometimes, transactions can be of an ULTERIOR type, where there is a secret message given as well as the obvious one. The response is usually aimed at the secret part of the stimulus. These are more sophisticated social interactions, involving often invisible exchanges such as flirting or bullying. These are the type of transactions that indicate we are getting into a psychological game. The sender puts out a superficially plausible message that carries with it a hidden

61

subscript. The recipient receives both messages, but responds to the secret one without acknowledging the socially obvious one. Both are in the grips of the transference & countertransference spell.

EXAMPLE of an Ulterior Transaction

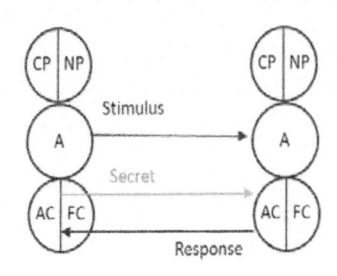

Stimulus: 'What did you do with my shirt?' A-A

Secret: 'You're always messing up my things.' AC-AC

Response: 'You're always having a go at me.' AC-AC

Ulterior transactions are the starting point for psychological 'Games'. The secret messages 'hook' us into a hypnotic spell, reading the intention behind the stimulus, resulting in us reacting in ways that we might later regret. Ulteriors are energy exchanges, not just data. They reveal invisible manipulations. Many of us find 'ulteriors' stimulating whilst others find them difficult, even overwhelming. They are in the realm of 'social skills', something some of us manage, others find too difficult. TA allows us to understand what is really going on when people talk together. It enables us to see how it is that we might go about repeating past discomforts with partners, friends, work colleagues or bosses. By making sense of how we might 'set ourselves up' it opens up exciting possibilities for change.

Strokes:

When you and I transact, I signal recognition of you and you return that recognition or vice versa. In TA language, any act of recognition is called a STROKE. People need Strokes to maintain their physical and psychological well-being. Strokes can be positive or negative, conditional or unconditional.

EXAMPLE: 'I hate it when you leave your socks lying about.' (Negative Conditional)
'I hate you.' (Negative Unconditional)
'I love your clothes.' (Positive Conditional)
'I love you.' (Positive Unconditional)

Some people are brought up on a 'diet' of negative Strokes and cannot easily accept positive ones. Parents who only Stroke a child for 'doing', rather than for 'being', may promote a later preference for conditional Strokes (i.e. performance).

Learning how to accept and reject strokes is a vital part of TA therapy as well as behavioural change. Many of us do not recognise the social politics of strokes. Being able to reject unwanted strokes (such as from someone who is sexually interested in you, but you not in them) is a social skill. Being able to tolerate rejection is another skill we need to learn. Once we are able to face disappointment, in the form of receiving a negative stroke, we increase our willingness to take social risks (such as asking someone out on a date). As we address our programming around our stroke diet, we become more assertive, more powerful human beings and release ourselves from the shackles of low self-esteem.

Time Structuring:

When we transact in a group or pairs, we use time in very specific ways. An analysis of how we spend time **with others** is called TIME STRUCTURING. There are six ways in which we structure time.

1. **Withdrawal** is not the same as taking ourselves off on our own. Instead, it is appearing to be involved socially, yet switching off – like being in a classroom while not paying attention to the teacher because we're off to the beach in our imagination! Sometimes we do the same thing at work or with our partner - 'the lights are on but there's no one at home'. We may be data processing, but we are avoiding social processing. Too much withdrawal and we are not feeding the need for social contact or spontaneity, too little and we are not making time for reflection and contemplation.

2. **Rituals** are actions that we engage in with others, that are repetitive and do not require thinking. Anything done ritualistically can have a social purpose (such as communal prayer) or serve to push down our feelings of anxiety (such as cleaning something that does not require cleaning). Obsessive-Compulsive Disorder (OCD) is an example of the latter, where the ritual has become meaningless in terms of interacting with other human beings. Whereas rituals are social, they involve little data processing and may not allow too much of the individual's personality to come through. Anything can be done ritualistically, including perfunctory sex.

3. **Pastimes** usually involve complementary transactions and 'talking about' topics that are either non-contentious (the weather, cars, fashion) or topics that have previously been done to death (the state of the planet, men, women). There is little useful data processing function. Its social purpose is to maintain social discourse and a sense of belonging. The individual's personality usually shines through, such as their sense of humour, mischief, seriousness etc. Social media is often a major source of pastiming and can become addictive, especially when it replaces all real social interaction with a virtual experience.

4. **Activities** involve us doing something together. The emphasis is on the doing, such as planning a project,

65

painting a room, engaging in a sport, gardening, watching a film. This can be a good source of strokes. However, this is not the same as having fun by playing and being intimate. Activities are more about participating in a 'doing thing'. Activities allow for social and data processing, but may suppress the personality in for example work. Hence the saying 'all work and no play, makes Jack a dull boy.'

5. **Games** are attempts at intimacy that go wrong. The guy misinterprets the gal's signals and goes in for a kiss when all she wanted was friendship; the underlying signals were ignored and/or misleading signals were sent. Games involve ulterior transactions so there is a much greater risk of experiencing crossed transactions. If a person is in the habit of re-experiencing the same painful pattern of behaviour, then this is the indication that he is hooked on games. Games are examples of our need for incident, repetition or of the individual's unconscious personality making an appearance.

6. **Intimacy** is about being able to be one's true self with another. This often involves honesty and being able to be vulnerable as well as engaging in close emotional, physical, spiritual and sometimes sexual encounters. Intimacy involves stripping away the mask and enjoying being the person you are with another who feels the same way. Unlike games, there are no crossed transactions.

Withdrawal -> Rituals -> Pastimes -> Activities -> Games -> Intimacy

——— Greater chance of getting Strokes ———→

——— Greater psychological 'risk' ———————→

An analysis of how a person structures their time can reveal a lot of information about the type of strokes they need to receive, and about the types of strokes, they need to give.

Strokes are ways of recognising each other, be it through non-verbal interactions such as touch or smiles, or verbal interactions such as saying 'good morning' or 'I love you'.
We each have our own 'Stroke Bank', and we structure our time to create our unique balance of Strokes. We manage our accounts by either **giving** strokes or **withholding** them from others, and by **accepting** or **rejecting** strokes that others give us. When we manage our accounts well, the psychological payoff is good (we feel good about ourselves and others), but mismanagement results in us feeling bad about ourselves and/or others.

The six Hungers:

Strokes are vital for our health – we are fundamentally social in our nature and require interaction with others to maintain our psychological, emotional, spiritual and physiological well-being. Berne recognised that we need strokes to fulfil 6 human hungers. These are hungers for:

Structure   Stimulus   Contact   Recognition   Incident   Sex

Structure hunger is satisfied by working, doing familiar things, eating familiar foods, engaging in rituals and pastimes. The importance of structure strokes is predictability and certainty. They counteract the anxiety that comes with feeling lost or without a purpose. However, Structure hunger strokes may make us passive and unwilling to try new things. We can become 'controlling'. Over-reliance on structure strokes may lead us to become 'workaholic' or 'institutionalised' since we depend on external timetables for our strokes. Think of 'formula feeding' babies after the war. Too few structure strokes and we may become chaotic, confused and disorganised.

Stimulus strokes are given/sought for being, seeking unfamiliar things, taking risks, having fun, engaging in activities such as sports or dating. Stimulus strokes may be pleasant or unpleasant. Stimulus stokes are riskier than structure ones, yet are often more rewarding. Over-reliance on stimulus strokes can result in us engaging in ever more dangerous pursuits in order to get the thrill. It can lead to recreational drug use, manic hedonism and burnout. Too little stimulus often leads to boredom, isolation and depression.

Contact strokes are given/sought to counteract loneliness, to experience the warmth of another, as well as for safety, love and connection. These strokes can be physical, emotional or spiritual in nature, and serve to remind us that we are not alone. Physical touch as well as being touched emotionally give us a sense of love and compassion. Over-reliance on contact strokes may result in us being dependent on others or having to be dependable for others, caught up in symbioses. It can lead to alcoholism, stalking or obsession with social media. Too little can lead to compulsive self-reliance

Recognition hunger is fundamentally about a need for acknowledgement. We need to know that we matter to someone else, that we belong, that our life has meaning and purpose. Whereas we need to know this for ourselves, we also need to hear it from significant others. Without recognition, we might feel rejected and end up taking things too personally. Over-reliance on recognition strokes usually occurs because we don't fundamentally recognise ourselves in the first instance. We try to compensate for this by relying on others to tell us how great we really are. It can lead to an ego-centric, low self-esteem individual who is desperate to plug into others who feed this narcissistic hole.

Incident hunger is provocative by nature, and involves the need to test relationships (sometimes to destruction). The person is acting out an internal civil war between different parts of themselves. For instance, a person who wishes to grow up and become independent may also wish to remain young and dependent. They may act grown up, but fail to land the interview that gets them the well-paid job. Alternatively, they may remain small and needy, but resent their friends who are moving on in their lives. Over-reliance on this type of stroke can lead to a person creating incidents – making mountains out of molehills – to keep their supply levels high. This can lead to a person who is hyper, unreliable, depressed, suicidal, always making excuses and difficult to be in a relationship with.

Sex is a complex hunger because it is related to so many other factors. For some, it is part of being in a stable partnership. For others, it is for comfort. Others relate it to power and engage in dominant-submissive encounters. For some it is casual whilst for others it is intense. For some, it is a product to be sold, whilst for others, it is about having children. For some it is about giving/receiving pleasure, for others, it is about giving/receiving pain. Over-reliance on sex strokes can result in meaningless encounters, engaging in demeaning practices and becoming obsessed with pornographic material. This can lead to a person who becomes cut off from their true sexuality, has identity issues and yearns for more sex in the vain hope of finding love.

Up to now, we have been exploring the external, public world. This is the world that we share. However, we also exist in a private sphere, a world described by the Structural model. This is the world of Being, a world of experiences, some our own, some the experiences of others.

The Structural model is more than simply three containers, Parent, Adult and Child. They are three states of mind, one based on our own history (Child), one on our experience of the history of others (Parent), and one based on a space within which we make sense of the other two (Adult).

We all were children once… and some of us regularly return to that state of mind. Some of us were so influenced by others that we adopted their state of mind and never a mind of our own. Some of us realised that there was another state of mind, one where we could process our own thoughts and feelings, remain sceptical and check things out for ourselves. This next section is about this internal world, its often-magical and sometimes strange experiences.

Life Script:

From the point of conception, we are susceptible to external world influences. Some of these influences are obvious and observable, such as the mother who takes out her frustration by physically beating her child or the teacher who dislikes the creative student and shames them in front of the rest of the class. Others are less obvious, such as the subtle signs of disapproval when the father feels threatened by his son's feisty nature or the sibling who is jealous of the prettier sister. Likewise, society exerts a significant influence, sometimes in the form of a backdrop – those born during the war years had to contend with scarcity and often developed a make-do mentality. Sometimes the influence was more direct - those born in a 'nice' village are less likely to expose the 'paedophile' who abused them for fear that they will expose the fact that the village was not so nice after all. These influences are exerted on us as we begin the process of growing up.

In TA there are at least 12 major influences or injunctions, which are restrictive, prohibitive sanctions that we hold unconsciously. Each of us may carry a number of these injunctions which are invisible constraints that influence and prevent us from reaching our true potential. They are very difficult to ignore, less alone break, and form the psycho-social programming we have all been subjected to.

Some are almost hard-wired and cause us great distress if we go against them, while others are less severe and debilitating. These Don't messages are:

Don't Exist **Don't' Be You** **Don't Feel** **Don't Think**
Don't Succeed **Don't Be Important** **Don't Be Well**
Don't Belong **Don't Be Close** **Don't Grow Up**
Don't Be A Child **Don't…**

Don't Exist is amongst the most severe injunctions. If it is held strictly, it may make the person commit suicide when it comes into play. When it is held less harshly, it may produce suicidal thoughts but no action. Held less severely still, it may make the person 'invisible' so that others don't remember their presence at say a party.

Don't Be You is an instruction to exist in your persona, to not be honest and to lead a double life. Many of us are uncovering this injunction as our Freedom of Speech is curtailed and we wish to appear virtuous, while privately hiding our true thoughts and feelings.

Don't Feel is an instruction to deny our private feelings, so becoming stoic and robotic. In the absence of feelings, we will find emotional displays distressing and struggle to be in an intimate relationship.

Don't Think is an order to ignore our private doubts and simply follow the instructions. It prevents us from individuating since we feel overwhelmed instead. A_2 is disabled and the person does not form opinions of their own. They are susceptible to indoctrination.

Don't Succeed prevents us from completing a task in its entirety. It kicks in whenever a person gets close to endings and produces sabotage and distress instead. Sometimes referred to as 'choking', it can create a stranglehold on the recipient's successful completion of projects.

Don't Be Important keeps the person hidden or invisible even when they succeed. They fear being in the spotlight and their anonymity being revealed. They prefer to work in the background and let others shine instead. Often the message received is: 'Don't be more important than ME!'

Don't Be Well is a prohibition on a person to be fit and healthy. Often the person experiences health issues that arise after traumatic events in their lives. This can take the form of physical restrictions or can morph into 'Don't be Sane' when mental health issues become evident.

Don't Belong is held by those that don't easily trust and make attachments. Often, they stay on the outskirts of groups and may experience symptoms of loneliness.

Don't be Close is a restriction found in those who fear intimacy. Closeness can refer to physical, sexual or emotional intimacy and those who have issues in touching or being touched by others.

Don't Grow Up keeps us from accessing A_2 and P_2. It makes us appear young for our age, like a Peter Pan figure. It keeps us needy and naïve like a society-programmed infant or slave.

Don't Be a Child keeps us out of C_2. It prevents us from having fun, being spontaneous and makes us over-responsible. Playtime is avoided as is anything unplanned.

Don't... is an open-ended prohibition. Whatever we're doing, we must stop. No questions asked. It has a paralysing effect on us when it kicks in, producing incapacitating confusion.

The injunctions are invisible influences that are passed on through the generations. Because they are non-verbal, we receive them almost as part of our DNA, as part of our inheritance. They are held privately and unconsciously, so they are in the province of the Structural Model of Ego States and the TA psychotherapist has to look more deeply to find them. They are not visible in terms of behaviour alone. Instead, they act to limit the person, like invisible chains or hidden programmes. They are often decisions made by our forefathers that still affect us.

For instance, Dad passed on a Don't Feel injunction to his son. Having lost his own father in the war, Dad learnt that by cutting off his own feelings, he wouldn't feel the pain. Dad's decision was Don't Feel, and this was passed unconsciously to his son. When his son was born, he had inherited the Don't Feel injunction which in turn would then be passed on to his children. The 'Don't feel' injunction affects many millions of us throughout the world and can often be traced back to losses suffered in the World Wars. Likewise, other injunctions that we receive as children, can be attributed to traumatic events or difficult circumstances (e.g. Potato famine) endured by our ancestors.

When we are very young, we all need to make decisions as to how to exist, to survive and how to get our needs met. These decisions are limited by the individual injunctions we each carry. Usually, between the ages of birth to five years, we make decisions about ourselves, about others and about the world we live in. These decisions are made at a time when the world is experienced through the eyes of a young child, not our grown-up view. We make sense of the world magically instead of through a more logical understanding. This 'Land of the giants' may appear friendly or hostile, and we adapt to the pressures of socialisation, to the demands made upon us by others, and find our own unique way of being in the world. We adapt as best we can to the world as we experience it AT THE TIME. These adaptations will affect our later beliefs, feelings and state of mind.

In adapting, each of us grabs hold of at least one of the following 5 antidotes to counteract the poison of the injunctions. These are called 'Drivers'. Unlike Injunctions, these are visible and we can observe them in action. They belong to the Functional Model of TA and are used by the behavioural Transactional Analyst to make sense of what the person is up to.

Be Perfect   Try Hard   Hurry Up   Be Strong   Please Others

Each driver is signalled by a distinctive set of gestures, postures, tones, words and facial expressions. They are typically displayed in less than one second and indicate that the person is in their script. TA handbooks often set out the details of these observable traits so I shall not dwell too long on them here.

Be Perfect is found in those that cannot own up to a mistake. They are typically over-responsible and looking for the 'perfect answer'.

Try Hard indicates that the person is persevering and won't let themselves be defeated. They tend to lose sight of the bigger picture and the 'other' in relationships.

Hurry Up indicates a high level of anxiety and an unwillingness to 'chill' and take things at a more reasonable pace. They often act faster than their thoughts can keep up with.

Be Strong is a stoic position, a stance where the person denies their own vulnerability. They often lead others because they remain stable when others lose their composure.

Please Others is found in those that entertain, make jokes or make light of situations that perturb others. They can be fun or become the butt of jokes or not take things seriously enough.

How does all this work? The injunctions weigh us down while the drivers buoy us up. As long as a person's drivers are followed, the injunctions do not come into play. However, under stress or in situations where the drivers fail, the injunctions make their appearance and distress is evident. That is usually the point when people seek help in therapy.

So, the person who has a Don't Feel injunction may cover it up with a Be Strong Driver. As long as the person is 'strong' (i.e. Not vulnerable) he will not feel the discomfort of his feelings. However, if for some reason he is no longer able to hold the Be Strong shield, he will expose the 'Don't Feel' injunction and will experience distress. Unable to 'feel' because of the injunction, the energy will not show in the emotions but elsewhere. Such a person may often develop unusual medical conditions such as 'skin rashes' or panic attacks. Usually, this person will experience themself, not as vulnerable, but as weak and judge themselves critically for being 'pathetic'. They will often live and work in an environment that equates vulnerability with weakness and does not acknowledge that all of us have a soft human core.

Another example is the person who has a Don't Exist injunction and covers it up with a Please Others driver. As long as the person pleases others the injunction is not in play. However, if that person does not please others (e.g. the comedian does not please the crowd), he will experience the Don't Exist injunction often in the form of severe depression or suicidal thoughts.

Adaptations such as these are decisional in that we decide how to best adapt to the injunctions we receive using our drivers. **These decisions are not based on thought.** They are instinctive, survival responses that are often irrational and held unconsciously. Based on these early decisions that we make, we create a narrative that forms the plan for the rest of our lives. This is called the LIFE SCRIPT, and it is a story of how life is going to be for us. For instance, are we going to have to work hard and struggle through life or are we going to have plenty and expect there is always going to be someone who will bail us out? This narrative is initially primitive and non-verbal. We 'write' the basic plot in our infant years before we are old enough to speak more than a few words. Revisions may be made to alter the details in later childhood and adolescence, but the basic plot remains the same. As grownups, we are no longer aware of this hidden programme or Life Script we have written for ourselves. Yet we are likely to set up our lives so that we move towards the final scene we decided upon as infants.

In SCRIPT ANALYSIS, we use the concept of the Life Script to understand how people may unawarely set up problems for themselves, and how they may set about solving those problems.

For instance, Sarah received a Don't Be Important injunction from her father and a Don't Think from her mother. She adapted by Trying Hard to Please Others such as her parents, teachers etc. (2 drivers). Her parents praised her and wanted her to do well. Yet, at the vital moment in exams, she blanked out and failed to deliver the promise that her teachers knew she was capable of. Under the stress, she was unable to maintain the drivers. She exposed both her injunctions – her blanking out is the Don't Think from mother, while her underachieving is the Don't Be Important (i.e. Don't Be more important than me) from father.

Left unaddressed, Sarah will be following her script. She will continue to falter at the vital moment. Through therapy, she may learn new strategies that update the original adaptation programme. She may even get to grips with the meaning of the original injunctions and trace these back through several generations. She can re-decide.

Injunctions are not simply the province of parents and family. Society itself often has a very profound influence on us. Seeing grown-ups in distress or frightened can lead us to adopt injunctions such as Don't Feel or Don't Be You. Likewise, we may adopt drivers such as Be Perfect or Be Strong to combat the anxiety that we experience in others around us.

Taking the Structural model a little further, we need to visit the world of Being and its foundation in Existential experience.

Frame of reference, Discounting, Redefining:

The way I see myself in the world, and the way I see others is my FRAME OF REFERENCE. The decision I made about myself and others, early on in my childhood, may be one of:

    I'm OK, You're OK   (Healthy position)
    I'm OK, You're NOT OK   (Paranoid position)
    I'm NOT OK, You're OK   (Depressive position)
    I'm NOT OK, You're NOT OK (Futility position)

This is my EXISTENTIAL position because it describes how I experience my existence in the world.

In order to maintain the validity of my original decision, I will need to ignore (DISCOUNT) or reinterpret (REDEFINE) a lot of what is happening to me, in the here-and-now as a grown-up, that may contradict this view I have of myself and others. I discount outside of my awareness. That is, I maintain my own particular blinkered view on life, as I have always done; by discounting in my own unique way. By discounting, I do not allow myself to see all the possible ways that are open for me to solve a specific problem. I may convince myself that I cannot solve it, or that only I can solve it, or that no one can solve it. In doing so, I confirm and reinforce my original existential position.

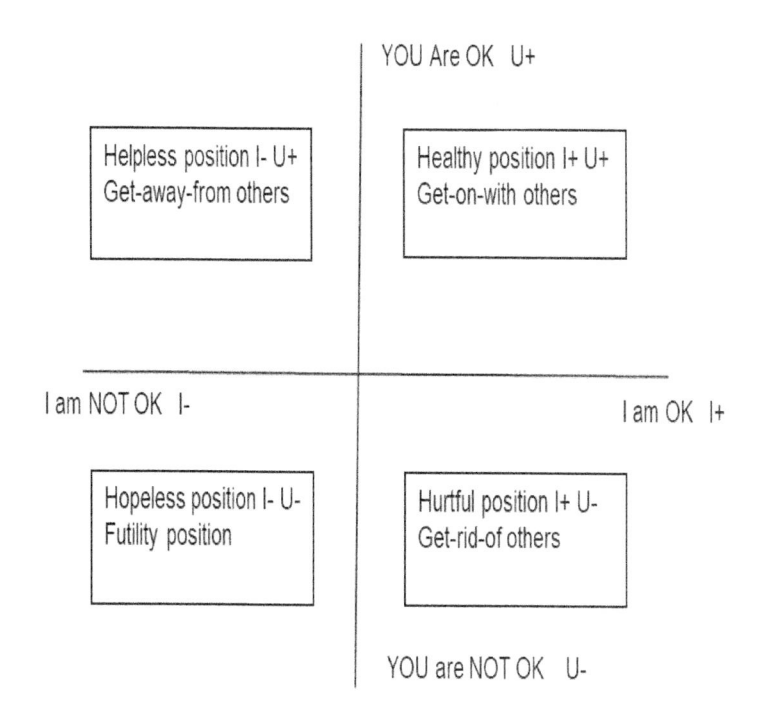

```
                         YOU Are OK  U+
                              |
  ┌─────────────────────────┐ | ┌─────────────────────────┐
  │ Helpless position I- U+ │ | │ Healthy position I+ U+  │
  │ Get-away-from others    │ | │ Get-on-with others      │
  │                         │ | │                         │
  └─────────────────────────┘ | └─────────────────────────┘
                              |
I am NOT OK  I-_____|_____ I am OK  I+
                              |
  ┌─────────────────────────┐ | ┌─────────────────────────┐
  │ Hopeless position I- U- │ | │ Hurtful position I+ U-  │
  │ Futility position       │ | │ Get-rid-of others       │
  │                         │ | │                         │
  └─────────────────────────┘ | └─────────────────────────┘
                              |
                         YOU are NOT OK  U-
```

The Franklin Ernst OK Corral model

We each have a favourite existential position, but we visit the others in our own unique dance.

For instance, Tom is in a restaurant and appears fidgety while watching others being served, knowing that they arrived long after him. He does not know at first that he is angry at this point, but is becoming restless and agitated. He starts getting hot under the collar. He pretends to himself that he is not bothered (Discount) and that the waiters are very busy this evening. He does not attract attention by calling a waiter and explaining that he has not been tended to since arriving. He does nothing to solve the problem. He then imagines that he is purposely being ignored (Redefine). His anger is turning into righteous indignation. How dare they! By the time a waiter arrives, he snaps in a rather aggressive way. Realising the shocked expression on the waiter's face, to his overreaction, he capitulates and ends up apologising.

Through applying TA, Tom realised that he had entered a game and was left feeling very uncomfortable. By discounting his initial feeling of anger, he did not take appropriate action. He escalated into rage, an annihilistic response rather than a problem solving one. His apology rescued the waiters from the fact that they did not tend to him properly in the first instance.

Tom's position started off as I am NOT OK, You are OK (I-U+) "the waiters are very busy tonight". It was a **helpless** position and he did nothing about the situation... other than to discount and ignore his growing sense of agitation. As he cut off his anger, he also cut off his options. He later became aware of the injustice of his situation as others were being served before him. Through redefinition of the problem, he skipped anger and went straight to righteous indignation, a rage response I+U- (**hurtful**). When he saw the shocked expression on the waiter's face, he realised he had overreacted and felt ashamed. He had entered the I-U-(**hopeless**) quadrant which was his final script position.

The transactional analyst helps the client become aware of his discounting and, in exploring options, to allow the solution of problems where the client has become stuck.

Each Structural Ego State contains a set of existential positions that may be very different depending on which Ego State is in charge at any given moment. Ego States are not simply content, represented by round, neat containers. These circles represent phenomenological experiences. We are fundamentally creatures of 'Being' not 'Doing'. We exist as Being-in-the-world-with-others, where the hyphens cannot be snipped as per Heidegger. This means that even in the internal world of the Structural model, we are connected to others. P_2-A_2-C_2.

This is nowhere more apparent than in our need to form relationships. Some relationships involve us compromising more of our Being than others. Nevertheless, finding ways of retaining some of our more precious attitudes and stances is necessary. Taking a no-compromising stance will limit our friendships and relationships.

We all exist in symbioses and this will be explored next.

Symbiosis:

In our infancy, we make a decision around dependency. Some of us choose to grow up and become more independent so taking charge of our own lives. An independent person retains their personal autonomy. Many of us though get trapped in dependency relationships, never releasing ourselves from these invisible shackles. Therapy should be about helping us to individuate and find our own voice, realising our full potential as grown-ups.

The dependency route is one where we rely too heavily on others. Staying dependent limits our life choices since we are tied to our source of strokes and sustenance. To a large extent, this decision on 'dependency' is based on how we interpreted our parents' actions or those who were important to us. We may for instance have learned that we got a lot of strokes for being little and needy, or for being serious and too responsible. We may then have decided to be dependent on or to be dependable for others. Either way, we get trapped. For us, this decision determines how we survive in the world. We establish with our parent figures an early SYMBIOSIS (you look after my needs, and I'll look after yours). Later on in life, we attempt to recreate this original symbiosis through psychological games.

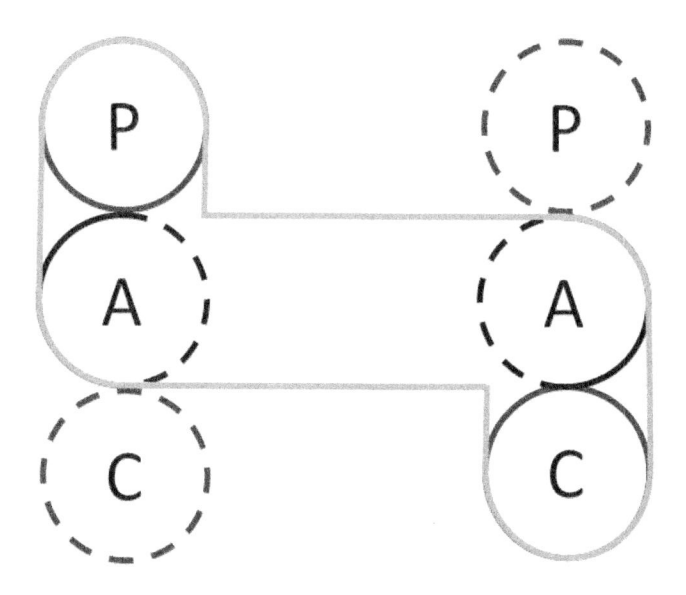

Developed by the author from Schiffian theory

Symbiosis is a **union of structural ego states** so that two or more people function as one. The person on the left contributes their Parent ego state while that on the right contributes their Child ego state. Each also contributes part of their Adult ego state, so that neither has a full Adult ego state available. This partial loss of Adult by both parties means that neither are fully present in the here-and-now and are in a type of spell or countertransference with each other. When asked a reflective-type question, they are apt to look at one another as if neither understands the question and each expects the other to provide the answer.

In addition to the degradation of the Adult, the person on the left has cut off their Child ego state, while that on the right has cut off their Parent ego state. This means that instead of a total of six ego states being available between them, three have been decommissioned.

Why is this significant? Surely a symbiosis is a useful way of dividing labour – she does the stuff in the kitchen and I entertain the guests? She does the ironing and I cut the grass!

This is not about dividing the chores. It is about HOW we go about making decisions. Do we do it from a Full Adult place each or from a Partial Adult place? In full Adult, I may realise that I'm opting for doing the grass cutting because I lack ironing skills. In choosing from partial Adult, I'm taking the more comfortable route and so avoid learning how to iron. In doing so I'm maintaining my dependency on my partner and avoid growing up.

In addition to a symbiosis degrading our Adult capacity, it also means sacrificing another ego state each. For instance, the Child ego state of the person on the left may be introverted and withdrawn, while that of the person on the right may be extroverted and expressive. By cutting off the Child to the left, the couple may come across as friendly and fun at parties. However, the person to the left may become depressed and drink too much as their Child receives no strokes, whereas the Child to the right hogs the limelight. Similarly, the Parent of the person to the left may be responsible and intelligent while that of the person to the right may be irresponsible and dull. The couple may come across as intelligent and responsible, but the person on the right may secretly harbour a shame of being uninformed or of harbouring ideas they dare not voice. They may be racist without really realising it or dull because they have never developed their inherited ideas. Once again, the excluded ego state does not receive strokes and the person on the right suffers as a result.

A functional symbiosis is not necessarily unhealthy whereas a structural one is. Just because a couple functions by dividing their chores, it does not necessarily indicate that there is a structural symbiosis. A structural symbiosis is indicated by the absence of a full Adult in each and the absence of one other ego state each. A three-legged-race approach to life!

Symbioses are what we attempt to re-establish in Rackets and Games. These stances limit our options and result in us getting caught in painful, repetitive and unhealthy patterns of behaviour. We shall examine these patterns next, their life-limiting restrictions as well as their potentially harmful consequences. Let's go back to the Functional Model:

Rackets:

"It reminds me of that old joke - you know, a guy walks into a psychiatrist's office and says, hey doc, my brother's crazy! He thinks he's a chicken. Then the doc says, why don't you turn him in? Then the guy says, I would but I need the eggs. I guess that's how I feel about relationships. They're totally crazy, irrational, and absurd, but we keep going through it because we need the eggs." Woody Allen in Annie Hall

Rackets, like that above, exist everywhere. They are based on a superficially plausible statement (social stimulus) such as: 'I have a problem.' This social level message is most often seductive. However, they also contain a more powerful message (psychological level stimulus) such as: 'I need the problem'.

The psychological level message will most often be coercive. In this case, it is: 'I need to have a problem'. The mistake is in trying to take the problem away by solving it! Here the Dr converts the racket into a game by suggesting a solution – we shall return to games later.

In America during the great depression, shopkeepers were subjected to what came to be called protection rackets. They were visited by mobsters who 'offered to protect them', from those who might wish to damage their livelihood, in return for a slice of their profits. Those who refused were later visited by the same mobsters who trashed their shops - 'should have taken the insurance!' The racket is, 'You need protection...... *from us*'. In this case, the coercive nature of a racket is obvious – 'choose to pay us...... *or we'll make you pay*'

A racket system is a self-reinforcing system of feelings, thoughts and actions, designed to maintain a contradiction or ambivalence within it. For instance, an organisation that markets itself successfully with a 'caring' image in the public eye, *whilst mistreating its workforce or suppliers in private.* Or a celebrity marriage that appears happy and committed, *while each partner is secretly having affairs.*

The TA concept of 'sweatshirts' captures this well. A sweatshirt often carries a message on its front. This contains the superficially plausible message. This is what we call the racket. *Yet on its back, it contains the psychological level message, often at odds with the former.* Each of us may carry ambivalent messages on our own sweatshirts. The first part of the message is the racket. It is the inauthentic, superficially plausible message; the message on the front of the sweatshirt. The second part (in italics), is its conversion into the game which lies in waiting

- the message on the back of the sweatshirt. Here are some examples:

You make me feel miserable……..*make yourself miserable to cheer me up*
If only I had more money/sex/time……….*and even then I'd still feel bad*
You're much cleverer than me…….*I'll show you clever*
We're so happy together……..*we can't stand each other*
Children nowadays have no shame……*shame I wasn't more carefree in my day*
Little boy lost………….. *I just don't want to grow up really*
I don't know what to do about………… *Yes but I'll reject all of your suggestions*
Why don't you?.......*please reject me for giving you advice*
I'm the perfect host……..*I need to keep feeling resentful and lonely by refusing your help*
I'm doing it all for you……*and you don't care about me*
I feel depressed………*more like raging inside really*
I have a pain in my body…….*and you're it!*
I'm sooo totally in love with you……….*well, myself actually*
Kick me……..*and you'll feel how awful I feel*
Schlemiel (mess maker) I'll mess up……..*and you'll have to forgive me*
Schlimazel (unfortunate) I'll get messed about by you……..*and have to forgive you*
You can depend on me……*to control you*

I'm committed……until I up sticks and run away
Let's……I meant you
I'm a beautiful princess……but you're not a patch on my daddy
I'm quite a catch……but you'll regret the day you caught me

Rackets systems often rely on racket feelings. In the case of the shopkeepers in America, the mobsters induced fear. The shopkeepers were more frightened of the mobsters than they were trustful of the law's ability to protect them. Not only were many of the cops and judges corrupt, but many of the shopkeepers were themselves acting outside of the law. In many cases, they relied on the same mobsters to provide cheap, illegal alcohol for them to sell on for a profit. Like the Woody Allen character, the shopkeepers had a problem, yet needed 'the eggs'. Racket feelings are often 'coercive' in nature. Unlike real feelings, they are designed to manipulate the other by making them feel bad.

A coercive feeling attempts to get the other person feeling uncomfortable since they feel blamed for it. Someone saying, for instance, 'you make me feel miserable' creates a feeling in the other person by blaming them. The other person now feels obliged to sort the problem out for the first: 'I'm sorry…I didn't mean to make you feel bad.' However, it is the second person who now feels bad and is left squirming. The first person has manipulated the second who now feels one-down and is open to doing whatever the first suggests.

A racket that has a seductive quality to it is 'If only... I had more money/a home/ a job, etc.' In its genuine form, it is what attracts people to give to charities. People are attracted to offering help to others who are in distress. In its racket form, it mimics the distress. However, the distress is not alleviated by any suggestions or offers of help. The need is not met or satisfied. Instead, the person remains unsatisfied – and the person offering help feels unappreciated.

Feelings that can be used for coercive purposes include: Depression, Tears, Rage, Anger, Guilt, Desperation, Anxiety, Helplessness and being Tired, Confused, Scared, and Hurt.
Rackets also involve racket beliefs. For example, a person saying 'you're much cleverer than me' is projecting a belief on another person. This is a set-up. Chances are that they secretly believe that they themselves are superior in some way.

Similarly, a projection can be onto a larger audience. The seemingly happy couple project this 'happy contentment' onto society often producing envy in others who believe they themselves are not as happy with their lot. Very often this is a sham, more energy going into appearing happy than actually being so. Think of Selma and Troy in the Simpsons episode 'A fish called Selma' where Troy says to Selma that even though their marriage is a sham, she will be 'the envy of every other sham wife in town'.

A very common racket is to look at the current generation of young people and find fault. The lack of some quality in young people such as shame often hides our secret wish that we had been allowed similar permissions in our day. This is only a racket if we secretly identify with narcissism. It is a genuine concern for grownups who question the future of society.

Sometimes we appear to be needing something when in essence, all we need to do is grow up. In 'little boy lost', the person appears to be lost and in need of directions. However, the person is not really after information, instead, they demand reassurance from others. This reassurance is that they don't have to grow up because we will intervene when they mess things up.

Linked to 'little boy lost' is the 'I don't know what to do about....' Racket. It allows the racketeer to experience a secret glee when they triumph in 'yes butting' all suggestions put to them by others.

A complementary racket of 'little boy lost' and 'I don't know....' is 'Why Don't You?' Here the person believes they can sort out the problems of others. While they relish their problem-solving skills, secretly they are after rejection, because sooner or later their ideas will be trashed.

Resembling 'why don't you?' in appearing to take care of others is the racket of 'perfect host'. Here the host/hostess takes great care to ensure that everyone is perfectly looked after, their every need met. Secretly, they are lonely (perhaps even resentful that no one else cares enough about them to look after them in the same way). However, they would never allow themselves to be looked after because they need to remain in control and keep others out, thereby maintaining their loneliness.

The martyr racket involves a person doing far more for another than is necessary or even requested. Having sacrificed so much for the other, the person holds a resentment because they secretly feel unappreciated. This resentment grows with every passing transaction, the person not taking responsibility for themselves and the proper budgeting of their resources. Often the martyr racket results in anxious depression. Unwilling to take the risk of expressing the growing frustration and resentment, the rage grows. This depression is simply a way of holding down the rage. It may become physiological as so much energy is needed to push down the deeply uncomfortable feelings. This describes the racket of anxious depression, not clinical depression, which is quite another matter.

With 'I have a pain in my body', the person may appear vulnerable and want reassurance. Yet, as opposed to someone with a genuine condition, they seem to get a lot of strokes for their ailment. People can structure a lot of time getting sympathy strokes, yet not do a lot to help themselves. That is because their condition imposes a racket belief that people must react with sympathy; surely only someone who is cold and uncaring would react otherwise? Secretly, however, they hold that others are the problem – 'you're the pain in my neck'.

The racket of 'I'm sooo totally in love with you' is very different to a genuine 'I love you'. ISTILWY is grandiose and often experienced in relationships where the person is projecting their ideal image of a lover onto the other person. Often, they haven't known each other for long enough to develop real feelings and what is termed love sounds more like infatuation. This relationship inevitably goes wrong when the 'lover' behaves outside of the projected version and does things that cannot be covered up by discounting and pretence. The person will no longer put up with their professed loved one and starts to look elsewhere for their next 'soul mate' (or 'sole mate' perhaps). Reality TV often promotes infatuation as real love.

Kick me involves someone saying or doing something that invites another to kick them. In its ongoing form, one person gets his 'kicks' from being kicked, the other from doing the kicking. It is a form of sadomasochism and is often played sexually, physically or emotionally.

Schlemiel is a racket where one person commits messy acts and says 'I'm sorry'. They expect (demand) forgiveness. For example, the clumsy waiter who keeps dropping food and wine on his customer. In order to be a successful racket, it requires the right customer. If the customer is a schlimazel (unfortunate) they will simply say 'that's ok' each time the waiter messes up. In time, this will convert into a game usually when either the schlimazel gets fed up or the schlemiel escalates to breaking point. The schlimazel will blame the schlemiel who will, in turn, appear hurt and innocent. The schlimazel will appear to have overreacted and offer an apology, whilst the schlemiel will accept the apology whilst secretly being gleeful. The example of Tom in a restaurant, given earlier, fits this description.

In 'you can depend on me', the person creates a dependency by not allowing the other to do things for themselves. For instance, a father doing all the DIY and not teaching his son how to do such work. When the son is older, he still needs his dad to do the DIY, and the father is controlling the situation by curtailing the son's independence.

The racket of 'I'm committed...' is different from the genuine thing. In a genuine commitment, the person stays with the difficult situation and whatever difficult feelings arise. The commitment is 'for good and for bad, in sickness and in health'. In the racket version, there is a get-out clause... 'I'll run away if I get uncomfortable.' Thus, the person avoids growing up by avoiding life's lessons.

In 'Let's...' the person appears to be acting as if they were part of a team. Only later do we discover that they have remained behind and left us to face the world alone. This could take the form of 'Let's... get married/commit suicide/you and him fight, etc.' In its racket form, 'Let's...' appears as an activity. Once the switch is pulled, it converts into a game.

One day, the Lone Ranger and Tonto were out on patrol when they came to a mountain pass. As they rode through the pass, the Lone Ranger noticed a large number of Indians looking down at them from the ridge above. He looked to the opposite ridge, and found it similarly populated. Glancing ahead and behind, he discovered the pass completely blocked by more Indians.

*"Well, Tonto, it looks like we're headed for some trouble,"
the Lone Ranger said to his faithful companion.
"What do you mean WE, white man?" came the reply.*

In 'I'm a beautiful princess...' the woman remains a pampered 'princess'. All she has to do is stay beautiful and be waited on hand and foot. She does not take responsibility for herself or her whimsical nature. When her needs are not met exactly and promptly at that, she may have a tantrum (switch) and compare her partner unfavourably to her perfect 'daddy'

In 'I'm quite a catch...' the initial appearance is deceptive. As the relationship proceeds, the person changes... they may become fat, violent, unpleasant or controlling. The initial presentation was just a front with which to hook the unsuspecting other. If the other person does the 'I'm loyal' racket, they may find it difficult to consider options other than to live a miserable life together.

Before we leave this subject, let's look at the bigger world picture. In 2008 we experienced a recession generally blamed on the banks. Their racket can be summed up as 'Too big to fail' TBTF. In essence, if enough financiers/banks act recklessly with the public's money, they coerce us into bailing them out. This fairly new racket is about 'privatising the profits whilst socialising the losses'. Few financiers have jumped from buildings as opposed to the great depression!

Likewise, some people borrow money that they cannot afford to pay back. In Berne's day, this game would have been called 'debtor' with its consequent uncomfortable payoff. In a modern world, however, there are so many people engaging in over-borrowing that the rules have needed to be changed. There is now a comparatively easy way out of debt – again TBTF has become part of our modern culture as the traditional uncomfortable feelings of guilt and shame and social disapproval are disappearing.

A S Neill v Erich Fromm!

A Racket is a way of behaving that is 'scripty'. It entails the person feeling a familiar childhood feeling, which is maladaptive as a grown-up means of problem-solving. These feelings are real enough; however, they are the result of us attempting to manipulate reality. Someone needs to end up NOT OK and we might achieve that by choosing to interpret events in certain ways or by setting up situations to justify the same end. **Psychological Rackets are engineered outside of our awareness by our unconscious self** and serve to keep us feeling, believing and behaving as we have historically done.

Those rackets that are consciously engineered are termed manipulations. For example, the salesperson may consciously manipulate us into buying goods by saying "it's the last one in stock." This is not a racket because it is conscious manipulation. It uses the same coercive or seductive techniques, but here the salesperson is consciously manipulating the customer.

Rackets are ways of being that we have grown used to in ourselves and are held unconsciously. We are unlikely to recognise our own rackets until they are pointed out to us by others, often painfully through psychological games.

Each racket is based on a scripty set of beliefs, feelings and behaviours. Feelings of **inadequacy, guilt, depression** and **rage** are racket feelings. They substitute for the real feelings that are buried deep down. For instance, a person feeling depressed may be hiding anger and self-loathing. Similarly, racket beliefs such as **life's unfair, why me? I'll never forgive** and **I don't need**, avoid us taking responsibility for ourselves as grownups. Rackety behaviour includes **addiction, exhaustion, psychosomatic ailments** and **antisocial acts**.

We learnt our rackets in childhood as we got stroked for rackety ways of being. Very often, real feelings may not have been encouraged or allowed in childhood, e.g. Anger, sadness or fear may have been prohibited. Parent figures may not have responded to a child in distress if the child showed anger, or may have reacted inappropriately, meeting anger with aggression. The child may then have decided to have another feeling instead, one which the parent-figure would permit. This might have been anxiety or guilt or helplessness.

Sometimes the child learned to engage in racketeering behaviour, such as committing antisocial acts instead of expressing vulnerability. For instance, a child may have learned to lie in a culture that punished honesty and rewarded deception. Or they may have learned to steal rather than ask for what they wanted, knowing that to take was considered preferable than to ask.

In other instances, the belief system is rackety. It may be that the person believes that all problems can be resolved through hard work (the Try Hard driver). In that case, the individual may believe that if only they engage in hard work their personal problems will resolve themselves or disappear. Another example is the belief that if we get things perfectly right (the Be Perfect driver) we will do such a perfect job that others will have to stand back and admire. We will not encounter conflict since no one could possibly complain and have a go at us! Such beliefs are often delusionary, yet we maintain rackety beliefs regardless.

Racket feelings would have covered up the real feelings and because they were stroked, the child would have learned to continue in this way. Similarly, racket beliefs and behaviours can be seen as a compromise, decided upon in infancy, in order to ensure the child's survival. As a grown-up, the person is not likely to easily let go of such decisions, making for habits that are difficult to break out of, e.g. Substance dependency, anxiety, losing one's temper, running away....

Racket feelings, beliefs and behaviours, attempt to mimic the real thing. Thus, the man covered in tattoos may give the impression that he is 'hard' and that others are better off steering clear of him. Yet the mimic may be a man who covers himself in tattoos, yet is sensitive and feels vulnerable. The tattoos serve the purpose of keeping others away.

The feeling of tiredness may bring sympathy from those who believe that the person must have exerted themselves or be under a lot of stress. Yet this presentation may disguise the feelings of rage that may reside within. As others are drawn into helping the 'tired' person, they could be accepting an invitation into a game – 'I'm tired of all you lot trying to help!'

A **real feeling** has a natural, healthy quality about it. Once expressed, the person can get on with his life. On the other hand, a **racket feeling** feels uncomfortably familiar, and tends to linger well after the situation that gave rise has passed. Because racket feelings are a substitute for the real thing, they do not satisfy or complete the experience. A racket is rather like picking at a scab; pain is felt, and another one grows in its place. Some people structure a lot of their time in such a way as to set up their familiar bad feelings. These rackets, whilst unpleasant and disagreeable, may nevertheless be paradoxically 'comfortable' because they are so familiar.

Games and Stamps:

Years ago, I came across a group of parents whose children had severe special needs. They were fervently discussing the fact that the school did not provide their children with a minibus, and that consequently the children were not taken out on trips. 'If only the school had a minibus' was the cry. Naively, I stepped in, having procured minibuses in the past from a well-known charity and said 'I know how to get a minibus for free'. Expecting to be greeted with thanks for solving the problem, there was stunned silence. Eventually, someone piped up, '… But we won't be able to afford a driver' and the conversation assumed its previous fervour. This was an example of a seductive-coercive racket 'the first person to attempt to solve the problem will be rewarded with… a group shun and be left with a sense of 'what an idiot I am'.

Games are an escalation of rackets. Whereas we can engage in rackets on our own… *we need at least one other person to convert them into games*. For instance, 'I'm a beautiful princess…' or 'little boy lost…' are rackets. They need a second person to convert them to into a game: '… you're not a patch on my daddy' or '… I just don't want to grow up really'. Like Rackets, 'Games' involve us manipulating reality so as to justify our own existential position. Unlike rackets, however, they involve a 'switch' or unexpected twist that often leaves us feeling confused. When the 'switch' is activated, the contradiction or ambivalence is revealed, and the racket is converted into a game. It is this surprise element that intensifies the negative payoff received at the end.

Vann Joines defined a game as "the process of doing something with an ulterior motive that:
(1) Is outside of Adult awareness
(2) Does not become explicit until the participants switch the way they are behaving, and
(3) Results in everyone becoming confused, misunderstood, and wanting to blame the other person."

Games start off with a 'Con', that is, a secret invitation to play. For instance, someone racketeering from a 'Little Boy Lost' position might say something like **"If only I could make up my mind what to do about my... job/house/spouse/children/holiday/life..."**
The secret message is *'I can't think for myself...'*

The second player, in accepting the invitation to play, replies with a 'Gimmick'. This might be something like **"Why don't you?"** or **"I'll tell you what..."** or **"Give it here."**
The secret message in this is *'I can do your thinking for you'*. As long as the two players continue to racketeer along the lines of *'I can't think for myself ..'* **(HELPLESS)** and *'I can do*

107

your thinking for you' (HELPFUL), each will be collecting strokes for their eventual payoff. They are in a symbiosis where the first player is excluding their Parent ego state, while the second player is excluding their Child needs. Each receives strokes that maintain their existential position.

However, if either player gets bored or tries to get out of the situation, the other player may pull the 'SWITCH' and turn the racket into a game. For instance, the 'Little Boy Lost' player may decide that he won't be told what to do anymore and cross the transaction by saying **'What gives you the right to tell me what to do?'** (HURTFUL). The other person gets into their **'I feel rejected'** (HURT) position. This stops the rackets and there follows a momentary period of confusion where the real-yet-secret intention of each player is out in the open. At the switch, the messages on the back of the sweatshirts come into play. This painful realisation of a 'trap' brings with it the intense negative payoff that is the hallmark of a 'Game'. The essence of a Game then is to experience intense negative strokes.

Each player then collects a STAMP, which is a bad feeling about self or others, which will serve to justify the person's rackety way of being. The game, therefore, reinforces our existential position as well as maintaining our original symbiosis. This particular game is sometimes called **'Why don't you….Yes but..'**

In his famous book, 'Games People Play', Eric Berne describes how we use games to set up our own favourite bad feelings. Stephen Karpman devised a DRAMA TRIANGLE to describe what happens in a Game. There are three roles in a game - PERSECUTOR, RESCUER and VICTIM.

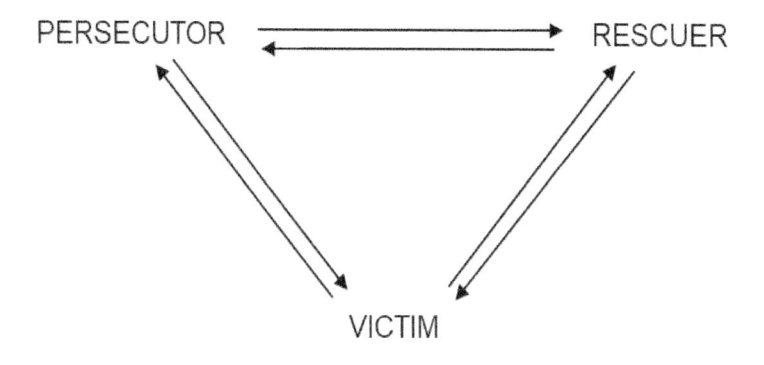

```
PERSECUTOR  ⟶  RESCUER
          ⟵
        ↖   ↗
          ↘ ↙
         VICTIM
```

The Drama Triangle (Karpman)

In a Game, the players take up roles at the start; in this case, **'Little Boy Lost'** (Victim), **'Why don't you?'** (Rescuer). When the switch is pulled, the players take up different roles; in this case, 'Little Boy Lost' becomes **'NIGYSOB - Now I've Got You Son-of-a-bitch'** (Persecutor). **'Why don't you?'** becomes **'I feel rejected'** or **'I was only trying to help'** (Victim). It is the 'switch' in roles that produces intense negative strokes. Because Games are played outside of awareness, the players experience momentary confusion as they move into their new roles. It is as if neither player had anticipated the (inevitable?) ending and its awaiting payoff.

So, what's in it for the participants and how come all of us succumb to games at some time? Games provide us with social and psychological advantages. When we play a Game role such as Victim or Rescuer, we are likely to get strokes, some positive some negative. However, those strokes keep us in script. In effect, we become dependent on similarly gullible people with which to play games and become slaves to societal programming. Games demand that we remain dependant and infantile in our search for crooked strokes.

Eric Berne famously said "don't ask 'am I in a game?', ask instead 'what game am I in?'"

Because games are played outside of our awareness, we are unconsciously on the constant lookout for partners who have complementary rackets. If our stroke balance is low, we may be vulnerable to invitations from others to play. Alternatively, we may be the ones that unknowingly initiate proceedings.

Games can leave us with very uncomfortable feelings, often accompanied by very uncomfortable beliefs about ourselves and others, as well as actions that we may well regret. All of these are negative strokes that quickly fill up our stroke account. Likewise, games can give us fake positive strokes and an artificial high based on conforming to the diktats of the group we belong to.

Played at a level 1, the strokes may be uncomfortable yet familiar and may fill up the stroke account just enough.

Say someone is playing 'I'm doing 80 mph in the fast lane – catch me if you can' (A form of 'cops and robbers'). The police may be playing the complementary game 'let's scare the stupid ****** - we'll not bother with a speeding ticket because the courts won't likely issue a fine'.

In this instance, the motorist is stopped and cautioned by the police. With adrenaline pumping, not knowing what the outcome will be (yet pretty secure that no further action will be taken), the motorist (Persecutor) becomes scared/excited to have been caught. He is now the Victim, being told off by the authority figure. The police have also had their thrill. There was no point in chasing after a motorist doing 80mph, knowing that they would not likely secure a conviction. Yet the flashing lights, fast car chase has also pumped them with adrenaline. Telling the motorist off has also relieved their boredom and filled their stroke account. The police have moved from the Rescuer to the Persecutor position on the drama triangle.

This is a level one game. The motorist and the police are likely to tell their story to someone else. It makes for good story-telling at parties and is likely to get a laugh and possibly builds up their status. The motorist tempted the dragon and then tamed it, while the police gave chase and then stopped the dragon. In an environment where there is an anti-establishment or anti-authority stance, the motorist can even appear 'sexy' – the one who is 'cool' and is not frightened to break the rules. They get stroked in this niche environment which keeps them in script as a subversive. However, it is a masochistic position, where the person puts themselves in harm's way and risks getting hurt.

The police may get strokes for re-establishing authority. Some of the strokes may be sadistic, however, since their real intention was to scare the *******motorist, a position more associated with glee than genuine protection. Once again, in the right environment, they get stroked positively and maintain their script position as heroes.

Yet, if a level one player meets a level two player, things can get more uncomfortable since a game is played at the level of the highest participant.

If say the same motorist doing 80mph encounters a car doing 100mph behind him, he may increase his speed to 100mph instead of moving to the slower lane and letting the other car pass. Both cars are now doing 100mph. The first driver is now in over his comfort zone but is getting strokes for not letting the other driver past. His adrenaline has kicked in and he is getting stimulus strokes. However, if he is now caught by the police, he is likely to face a fine and a likely ban on his licence. The strokes have escalated and he may not wish to tell his mates that he cannot drive, because getting caught may make him appear stupid. This is not such a 'sexy' prospect. He has been caught and neutered! The game was played at level two, the level of the driver in the second car. The level two driver may well have spotted the police car from afar and pulled back, avoiding getting caught. After all, they are experts at playing at this level. Thus, the game was played at level 2 and the payoff was far more intense.

At level three, games are played in a far more intense way, often resulting in tissue damage, ending up in the courts, hospital or morgue.

Thus, our driver encounters a driver doing 130pmh behind him. The driver of the second car is driving dangerously and recklessly and may have either stolen the car or is high on drugs and alcohol. Should our driver attempt to play, he is the one who most likely ends up crashing, since he is not used to this level of game playing. He is likely to end up in a hospital, possibly taking others with him, or may end up in the morgue. The driver of the second car may end up escaping prosecution since the police are having to deal with the scene of carnage left in the wake of this level three game.

This then leaves us with a frightening prospect. We all play games, yet whereas we can decide whether to play or not, we do not determine the level of the game alone. It is determined by the level of the most dangerous player. What may start off as a titillating encounter may become dangerous, even devastating. Remember Glenn Close in 'Fatal Attraction'?

Games are the 'snakes and ladders' of human interaction. Whenever we experience intense highs or lows, we are, in all likelihood, in a game.

Games are irrational, hurtful and destructive of loving, caring relationships.

When relationships work well, there is intimacy. An intimate relationship is an interpersonal relationship that involves physical or emotional closeness. Physical intimacy is characterized by romantic or passionate attachment or sexual activity. Emotional intimacy involves sharing one's feelings and being empathic to the feelings of others.

This is a shared, pleasant experience where the STIMULUS is POSITIVE.

When relationships break down, intimacy is replaced by psychological games. Games are a source of NEGATIVE STIMULATION. They can leave us feeling frustrated, depressed, anxious, worried, hurt, unappreciated, raging, suicidal, homicidal, crazy...

Games are emotional switches and contradictions that leave us feeling bad.

Can we stop playing games?

Not easily once we're in them because to step out is to risk triggering the switch leading to the payoff. Thus, unless we take the early payoff of bad feelings, we may remain in the game, building up to a more intense payoff at the end. We may try our hardest to keep the rackets from turning into a game. Yet if one of the participants starts to get bored or believes that the other is about to jump ship, this may be enough to trigger the switch.

Going back to the example of the level two car driver, should he realise that he is doing 100mph and has not given way, he may then decide to move over. The second driver, in going past him, may well indicate that he considers the first driver a 'chicken' or gesture something sexual, a signal that 'you're not really a man, after all, are you?' The first driver has not been caught by the police but is unlikely to boast to his friends. He is not going to get 'sexy' points for pulling out. He has pulled out of a level two game but is experiencing bad feelings. However, he has retained his licence and avoided a fine.

We can become addicted to getting our strokes by playing games. The same driver may, minutes later, return to the 80mph game, hoping to entice a level one player. Giving up old habits is hard work, especially if we remain convinced that ... 'we are not in a game/the bad feelings aren't that bad really/that's life/everyone plays games/I can't stop/I would like to stop but...'

One of the aims of TA is to enable the person to get in touch with their real feelings and to express these healthily. Given the motivation to learn and determination to give up on their script, a person can learn to structure his time so as to produce good strokes for his real feelings. He will then give up the old destructive patterns, replacing them with authentic, satisfying ways of being.

The integrated Adult:

The concept of Life script implies that we are all programmed, to some extent. Childhood experiences, and our own early decisions based on these, lead us to follow a predetermined course in life. Our very sense of Being is compromised unless we reach a state of 'Authenticity'. This is the degree to which our actions are congruent with our values and desires, despite external pressures to social conformity. Our internal and external worlds need to reach a state of congruence - that neither degrades us nor degrades others. The 'Integrated Adult' is the destination aimed for in TA therapy; an authentic human being who is open to the views of others while remaining true to his own essence of being; willing to compromise where needed yet retaining his conviction where necessary. To do that successfully, we need to develop an understanding of Games and Script.

Games are the lifeblood of our script – like scenes in a play. To realise our full potential as grown-ups, we need to update the strategies for dealing with life that we decided upon as infants. When we learn that the old strategies are no longer working for us, we need to replace them with new ones which do work. In TA language, we need to move out of script and gain AUTONOMY. It implies the ability to be authentic, respectful and solve problems using the person's full resources as a grown-up. In so doing, we achieve independence.

TA is not about being constantly in Adult. Having the Adult in charge of every single decision would be exhausting. The aim of TA is to enable the individual to engage the most appropriate ego state at any given moment, be it Adult, Parent or Child. The choice of which is the most appropriate ego state in a given situation is best made by the Adult since by definition, this is the part of the individual concerned with the here-and-now. Sometimes it might be quite appropriate for someone to engage their Child or Parent Structural ego state. Someone having fun at a party, for instance, might engage their Child ego state and 'let their hair down', much as they did as a teenager. Or at the same party, they might engage their Parent ego state, becoming responsible for ensuring everything runs smoothly, in a way that their parents may have done. Alternatively, if they had to be serious and responsible in their childhood, their Child ego state might be serious and their Parent ego state, carefree. Ideally, the Adult ego state would seek to balance the needs of oneself with those of others, so that C_2 and P_2 are engaged appropriately. For instance, at a party a person might experience fun and be carefree, while also being available to take appropriate action should there be a need to deal with a serious matter.

The Adult needs to be able to distinguish between what is beneficial to the individual, and what is a racket. The idea of having the integrated Adult in charge sums up the eventual aim of TA. That is the Adult ego state that has access to the beneficial parts of both Child and Parent ego states. Therapy involves updating Child and Parent ego states so that the old data is filed away and replaced by redecided information. Muriel no longer throws a tantrum when things don't go her way. Instead, she has learnt how to be assertive. Adam no longer pushes people away with homophobic rants. He has accepted that sexual identity comes in many forms and varieties. The old information has not been destroyed, simply stored away and decathected.

With the integrated Adult in charge, the person is able to problem solve in the here-and-now and respond rather than react to situations. TA psychotherapy aims to mobilise the resources already present within the person, enabling him to make the behavioural changes he wants to make, thus allowing him to become the authentic person he has the potential to Be.

PART THREE

The Mind Revolution – the world we inhabit

Introduction

When I first wrote 'A Brief Introduction to Transactional Analysis' in 1992, the world was still largely a modernist one; one that had developed from the Enlightenment, where 'common sense' ruled. There was, however a competing narrative at work, especially in the United States. This different way of interpreting things has come to be called postmodernism. Originating in countries in Europe, such as Germany, France and Italy, it spread first to American universities and started to affect the way professionals in the humanities viewed the world. Its seductive assertions led many to set aside their previous conceptions of the world and to accept a radically different way of thinking. Consequently, in the USA - the birthplace of TA - there were only a handful of TA practitioners left in 1992, where there had been thousands the decade before. Although at this point the TA movement was still growing in Europe, the effects of postmodernist thinking were being felt and TA was starting to appear dated.

In this third part, 'The Mind Revolution', I have explored the rise of postmodernism as well as its fall. It is a more personal account and uses examples from my own journey to illustrate the changes evident in individuals and society. While I do not set out to deliberately offend or incite, my views will undoubtedly provoke some push-back, especially from those invested in political ideology. Eric Berne's work was always controversial, yet relevant to the times he lived in. However, times have changed and something has clearly gone wrong with the hope that people change for the better. This is no longer simply a push for Civil Rights for everyone. In the third decade of the twenty-first century, some groups continue to push for even more rights for themselves, while simultaneously denying the rights of others. Why is that and how do we put it right? Exploring that question is the purpose of this section.

My stance in writing this section is to remain authentic. I do not expect you to agree with all of my views. All I hope is that I get you to THINK for yourself. In doing so, I invite you to stay alert to contradictions, be aware of those who attempt to force you to see things their way and to remain sceptical. We live in a beautiful world full of happiness as well as pain and suffering. I pray that we find a way to coexist and evolve naturally as a free people, leaving a world fit for our children and grandchildren.

Because of the overly politicised world we currently inhabit, I thought it best to declare my hand at the outset. In every political-compass test I have taken, I come out as dead centre. I am neither Left nor Right in orientation. Despite having strong opinions on most issues, I am neither Authoritarian nor Libertarian. This I have always considered a strength as a Free Thinker and as a psychotherapist. Nowadays, however, it may be viewed differently by political purists. I believe in people, but I do not worship humanity. I respect the rights of people who believe in a supernatural God and those who do not. However, I challenge those who consider themselves to be atheists, as to whether they believe in secular Humanism as a religion? Be prepared to be challenged should you decide to read further...

My personal awakening

I was in Edinburgh for the International TA conference, feeling optimistic and excited. I had been given a ticket for the Live 8 concert taking place on 6th July 2005. The University campus where the conference was being held, was full of faces I recognised, as well as lots of tall, burly policemen who were also staying in residence. Those I spoke to told me that they were part of the Rapid Response Force and many had been sent to Edinburgh from London. They were there to police the G8 conference that was happening at the Gleneagles Hotel. I thought no more of it at the time. On the evening of 6th July, I spent a great evening at the concert. There was a festive atmosphere, everyone enveloped in a 'peace and love' feel. I spoke to many in the crowd and we were all on the same page. There was an innocent feel of John Lennon's 'Imagine' in the air. We sang, cheered and clapped the many entertainers who were giving freely of their time...and then the first thing happened that disturbed me...

Eddie Izzard took to the stage and said excitedly, "We've won it. We've got the Olympics coming to the UK!" Then there was a period of silence, followed by a deafening chorus of boos from the largely, Scottish audience. The atmosphere changed from that of 'One World', to a hatred of anything 'English'. At that moment I came out of my spell, realising that tribal, National differences had trumped the ideology of 'Togetherness'. Eddie Izzard initially struggled to keep the audience from becoming hostile, yet being a consummate professional, he ended up with everyone singing 'Flower of Scotland'. However, I was left disquieted by the hatred towards 'the other' I had experienced in the crowd. It was as if the shadow had just revealed itself from behind the veneer of tolerance and togetherness. The crowd's 'innocence' had disappeared so suddenly as had my personal sense of safety.

Much worse was to come, however. The next day, 7/7, I saw TV news reports of a bombing campaign in London, carried out by the now infamous group of extreme Islamist terrorists. As I watched in horror, as a nation wept, the thought occurred to me that it was no coincidence that the bombers had chosen that date to carry out their plot. For, while the streets of London were left unprotected by the Rapid Response Force being deployed to Edinburgh, the terrorists used that fact to carry out their atrocities. I was sickened by the realisation that while we were out enjoying ourselves, and protesters were occupying the police, the bombers were allowed free rein. That there had been some level of coordination and planning was evident. I had a growing realisation of just how much cunning and Hatred exists within the illiberal forces amongst us. That our naivety had been used as cover, under which the shadow had once again emerged.

I did not know then what I know now. That the 'peace and love' alliance contains many illiberal voices within it; that postmodern thought has 'switched off' many of us to the real dangers in the world. I had become AWAKE to a world that looked a lot uglier, more malicious and less safe than I had let myself imagine...

In the 'The Mind Revolution,' I aim to show how postmodernism has kept us blind to its real agenda; to lead us on a Pied Piper walk to the end of our personal freedom and individuality.

A New Religion

What we are nowadays experiencing, amounts to a cultural revolution; a politically-led movement that taps into the felt need in people to be good, and turns it into a religious fervour. History teaches us that once people believe that what they are doing is for the good, they are willing to turn a blind eye to what is actually going on in the name of their religion. And there is such a religion. Yuval Harari in his bestselling book 'Sapiens' calls 'Humanism' a religion, where Humanists worship Humanity instead of a supernatural God.[27] Many self-professed atheists are actually Humanists without having realised it. And the danger is the same as with traditional religions – dogma or rigidity of thought.

'Religions' give people a cause, such as to make the world a better place. For instance, Global Warming, Veganism, Nuclear disarmament, the European Union, Freedom of the Press. Even more than that, they give people an enemy to pour hatred into, such as Trump, Nationalism, Systemic Racism, Toxic Masculinity, Guns.

Likewise, modern party politics attempt to give us a binary choice - to side with the good against the bad. If you're not on the virtuous side, you're bad! In religious or political fervour, there is no room for dissent or question. There is no sceptical Adult ego state. Instead, 'You're either with me,

---

[27] (Yuval Harari, 2015)

or you're against me'. This is tantamount to 'Groupthink'[28], a 'herd-mind' where you are required to chant and believe whatever you're told by your side.

A wise client of mine once said in the nineties, "You only have a real choice if you're faced with at least three options. Otherwise, you are forced to choose between the devil and the deep blue sea, or between a rock and a hard place." This makes a great deal of sense since a binary choice is no ADULT choice at all. It is tantamount to coercion, and that is what religions such as politicised humanism force upon us. "What do you mean you don't side with us in our campaign to get rid of X? Don't you care about humanity?" This is really a political statement under the guise of Humanism's god. In TA terms, a Racket. The fact that I might disagree with X does not mean I wish to get rid of it. I might wish to explore it first, to fully understand its development and history, to see its function, to appreciate the felt need at the time when it came to be. I might decide that it needs to be intelligently reformed instead. I might decide that I want to keep it after all. I don't simply wish to appease the promoter of the all-or-nothing message by appearing virtuous.

We are witnessing a concerning trend in society today, namely the silencing of dissenting opinions and the

---

[28] (Christopher Booker, 2020)

punishing of those who hold them. Should we not instead be encouraging different voices and engaging in debate? It is not virtuous or moral to wish to purge inconvenient opinions or narratives from our culture no matter how 'right' we believe ourselves to be. For that is the path of religion and righteousness. It is puritanism.

This is not about morality, but it is about puritanism.

Puritanism is an illiberal and extreme religious ideology that originally sought to remove all traces of Roman Catholicism from the Church of England. It sought to convert others to its cause through a process akin to modern-day 'unconscious bias training'.

According to Bremer[29], there were 4 stages to conversion. First, a **preparatory phase** designed to produce contrition for sin through introspection, Bible study and listening to preaching. Secondly, **humiliation**, when the sinner realized that he or she was helpless to break free from sin and that their good works could never earn forgiveness. After this, the **realization** that salvation was possible only because of divine mercy—Finally, **justification**, when the righteousness of Christ was imputed to the sinner and their minds and hearts were regenerated. For some Puritans, this was a

---

[29] (Francis Bremer, 2009)

dramatic experience. They referred to it as being born again. It is also a recipe for 'Radicalisation'.

The same 4 stages are present in a cult conversion. Conversion is a cathartic experience that brings up powerful emotions and leaves us feeling vulnerable – and therefore susceptible to psychological manipulation. It exploits the fact that once made to feel vulnerable, people desperately grab onto whatever is on offer. **Desperation is a state of intense anxiety, felt by some as if they're going to burst.** Once desperation sets in, it leads to a panic that defies all logic. It is at the point of desperation that cult leaders offer a cure to the intense anxiety. All someone has to do is renounce their previous life and have their hearts and minds regenerated. Once they 'take the knee', they experience relief and are reminded of their new, 'better' belief system by the rest of the cult members. People have not come to their new beliefs through education or individuation. Instead, they are forced to believe the new edicts or 'swallow them whole' without scepticism or question. From then onwards, this is their 'new normal'.

This is indoctrination. It replaces education and uses a clever mix of seduction and coercion to force people to accept the creed.

Indoctrination or conversion can sometimes occur in therapy; in cases when therapist bias creeps in and turns a client-led process into a therapist-led one - where therapy stops being a healing experience and becomes corrupted. In such instances, instead of helping a person discover their own mind, the mind of the therapist is inserted as a better version. I believe that modern reformulations of 'therapy' pose such dangers to naïve and unsuspecting clients. We must not lose sight of the fact that puritanism believes in an I+U- existential position rather than an I+U+ one. **Therapists are NOT better people than their clients, nor do their clients become 'better people' as a result of therapy.**

Puritanism's underlying belief is in the 'moral superiority' of some people over others. It believes in 'purifying' that which it considers bad or evil.

The Nazi regime adopted puritanism under its programme of 'Lebensunwertes Leben' or 'Life Unworthy of Life', thereby condemning Jews, Romani Gipsies, the disabled and other groups it considered as 'useless eaters'. This is a vile and dangerous belief to hold, since historically it has led to incarcerations, torture, exterminations and genocide. Mao's cultural revolution, Bolshevism and Nazi Germany are examples of such movements.

Puritanical beliefs are often fanatically held. They go contrary to my core principles and the reason I became a Transactional Analyst in the first place. I believe that I am no greater or lesser a person than you, only different. You are entitled to your religious beliefs and so am I. You have no right to burn me at the stake and neither have I the right to burn you. This is the true meaning of the I+U+ existential position in TA. You might not like me and I might not like you. Nevertheless, we each deserve the right to inhabit this planet and make of our own lives what we will. Those of us that got behind the Civil Rights movement in the 1960s fought for freedom for all, not just for puritans.

The nature of belief

I have strong beliefs in many things and I also like to challenge myself, through reading, self-reflection, introspection as well as dialogue with family, friends, clients and colleagues. I enjoy rigorous debate and am open to being presented with views that challenge my own. I have changed my opinion on many things, yet have retained most of my beliefs. For instance, I believe more in traditional values such as compassion, kindness and patience than I do in modern formulations such as diversity, empathy and equality.

So, what is belief and how does it differ from an assertion, an opinion or an attitude? In epistemology, philosophers use the term "belief" to refer to attitudes about the world which can be either true or false. The question then is who decides what is true? How is it decided?

Going back in time, witch trials decided what was true. During medieval times, religion was revered as the source of goodness and truth. Christianity dominated our culture and the ruling class dominated us with religion. It was an oppressive ideology that allowed the aristocracy to laud it over the peasants. It was a Master/Slave dynamic. Laws were originally designed mainly to benefit the wealthy and protect their land and property.

Then came the Age of Enlightenment and the scientific revolution. Science allowed the 'truth' to be defined separately from the dogma of religion. It allowed the peasant to become educated and some became wealthy. As religion dwindled in power so did the aristocracy. Laws were redesigned to protect all people and we ushered in an age of liberty, individuality, constitutionalism and the rights of man. Many welcomed the end of the religious era and saw science and education as heralding a better future. I too held that opinion, an optimism for man's liberation from the oppressive forces that had made him a slave.

What was less obvious to me as I studied science, was that the vastly rich and powerful (the plutocracy), aimed to take over and duplicate the powerful role of the aristocracy, thereby creating a new peasant class. I was naïve and my opinion changed when I saw how people were being switched off to real threats and were being distracted onto imaginary dangers instead. Postmodernism is the ideology behind the new religion, or 'opium of the people.' It aims to do what traditional religion did before it - to usher in a new age of oppression and slavery - to end our individuality, to constrain us against our will, to limit our liberty and to challenge the idea that we are all equal under the law.

Using assertion instead of evidence, science that is not scientifically sound, government by decree and by feeding fear into the population, we are being tricked into giving up the very freedoms that our ancestors gave up their lives to protect.[30] The Right to Free Speech has been removed by the arrival of a sinister concept of 'hate speech'. Imported from a religion that does not allow scrutiny or ridicule, many have been persuaded that some things are off-limits. Restricted speech has returned, just as in the medieval, church-dominated period, when Galileo was condemned for saying the wrong thing. **Society is returning to a pre-enlightenment age, going backwards not forwards**.[31] The plutocracy promotes postmodernism as the way towards a progressive evolution of man. Instead, it is a way of returning us to an age when we were all obedient slaves. Meanwhile, unelected elites use their power and influence to rule from the shadows, from the corridors of power.

My attitude is still one that abhors violence and coercion, yet I do not believe in passivity either. I remain resolute in my belief in the future of humankind as a free people. I continue to use my skills to expose lies and deception under which many of us live our lives. That is my belief, my faith and what I have always fought for. We will need to delve into many areas that postmodernism has corrupted to make sense of the world we now live in.

---

[30] (Friedrich Hayek, 1944)
[31] (Joel Kotkin, 2020)

The questioning of reality

In Part Two, I showed that we each inhabit a private and a public world. The Functional Model applies to the **public world** we share with one another. This is the world that extroverts prefer to spend their time in. It is the world governed by behaviours; where we interact, work, form relationships, start families, have children, throw parties and try to get along. As grown-ups, we sometimes get to vote for those who govern us and establish a social contract that guides how we relate to one another. Usually, people abide by 'the golden rule' or the principle of treating others as you want to be treated. As people, we are governed by the Law of the land. We are allowed to do whatever we wish unless it is explicitly prohibited by Law. This form of freedom, traditionally enjoyed in the West, can be called Negative Freedom[32]. This libertarian position is based on concepts such as truth, knowledge and reason. The Enlightenment gave rise to this way of thinking. Following these principles, we arrive at 'common sense' based on objective truth. This traditionalist view is what many of us understand and live our lives by. However, there are new forces at work that curtail our traditional freedoms and the public world in 2020 is now very different from the world of

---

[32] (Isaiah Berlin, 1958)

last year. To fully understand these changes and how they have come about we need to enter the second world...

In TA, the Structural Model describes the **private world** of the individual, especially the Child ego state (C_2), which is a very personal experience. Introverts spend a lot of time in this 'inner' or private world. Unlike the more objective public world, C_2 is an imaginary, subjective experience and does not necessarily follow the rules of reason. The thinking is often best described as 'magical' and is sometimes infantile. In this private world, feelings often get the better of reason and thought, since logic has not been sufficiently developed. Too often it is fantasy, an egocentric experience and 'all about me'. For some of us, this private world contains many resentments and grievances, sometimes as a result of lapses in love and care in our upbringing. As children, we can choose to believe whatever we wish, to imagine without limits. As we grow up, however, this 'inner child' world (C_2) becomes counterbalanced by the thinking in the mature Adult (A_2) and the variety of content in a full Parent ego state (P_2). We learn both to self-reflect in A_2 and to access a wide range of ideas and opinions in P_2...at least we did until postmodernism arrived on the scene.

Before the arrival of Postmodernism, a succession of mainly continental philosophers challenged the Enlightenment's idea of 'Universalism' or there being a 'universal truth'.

Hegel[33] argued, in his famous concept of the 'Dialectic', that the very existence of thought contradictions showed there was more than one truth; later developed by Marx and Engels in their 'Communist Manifesto'[34]. Nietzsche spoke out against the Master/Slave dialectic that he saw in religion. Instead, he argued for a new man, a superman or 'Übermensch',[35] as the goal which man should aim for.

Nietzsche introduced the French word 'Ressentiment',[36] a mixture of resentment, blame, and jealousy. He saw Christian morality as grounded in ressentiment because it was the religion of the slave people, who were full of hatred and self-loathing. However, whilst Nietzsche wanted mankind to move beyond ressentiment, the modern Left has adopted it as its mantra, and in so doing has lost its way.

It was left to one of the 20th century's most brilliant minds to land the final blow on 'Truth'. Martin Heidegger's critique[37] of Descartes' 'I think, therefore I am', discredited the corresponding conception of truth and fractured the foundations of modernist philosophy. By "...regarding the *ego cogito* as the guarantor of its own continuing existence and as the basis of all things, Descartes reduces all entities to ideas or representations whose validity is

---

[33] (Georg Wilhelm Friedrich Hegel, 1807)
[34] (Karl Marx & Friedrich Engels, 1848)
[35] (Friedrich Nietzsche, 1883)
[36] (Friedrich Nietzsche, 1887)
[37] (Martin Heidegger, 1927)

determined by the rules imposed on them by the subject ego."[38]

Heidegger's concept of 'Being' as a phenomenological reality, that existed outside of Cartesian logic, led to Berne's concept of Structural Ego States. This embodied truth existed as a felt personal experience – what the Structural model in TA depicts as 'internal' or personal, subjective reality; as opposed to the more objective reality of the shared 'outer world' Functional model.

The assertion that 'all truths are subjective,' quickly became popular as a slogan. The interface between the personal, more subjective Structural model, and the shared, more objective Functional model was poorly understood amongst TA practitioners and TA suffered as a result. This flaw opened the floodgates for Postmodernism.

Postmodernists arrived and explored the internal world of the Child (C_2). This subjective, fantasy world was not simply explored, however. It was elevated in status. For many questioned the traditional understanding of what constitutes Reality. They were faced with the same philosophical crisis as traditional religion was in the late 1700s; namely, the reason, fact and logic arguments that arose from science and philosophy did not concur with those from theology. This religious crisis was resolved by

---

[38] (Abraham Mansbach, 1998)

Kant[39]; he downplayed logic, reason and facts and elevated 'faith' to paper over the cracks. Thus, the theological reality was preserved by elevating faith over reason, fact and logic.

The same sleight of hand trick was carried out by intellectuals who were invested in socialist ideologies. Faced with the collapse of socialist models such as National Socialism and fervently opposed to Western 'enlightenment' values, they were facing the same crisis. Instead of giving up on socialism, their solution was to downplay reason, logic and facts and to elevate human sentiments and feelings. Thus, the 'felt sense' that socialism was good and true trumped the facts and logic argument. This 'felt' version or 'perception' of reality underpins the whole postmodern movement.

Reality for them was not then to be found in facts, reason and logic (i.e. the Adult A_2). Instead, they believed that human sentiments and emotions are the true Reality. That the fantasy, private world of C_2 was 'the Truth'. The philosopher, Todd May, quotes Michel Foucault as stating, "It is meaningless to speak in the name of— or against— Reason, Truth, or Knowledge."[40] This goes against all common sense. Truth has become a matter of perception. Therefore, it follows that the public world we all share must be an illusion, a shared perception; that the external world

---

[39] (Immanuel Kant, 1781)
[40] (Todd May, 1993)

is based on nothing more than 'social constructs'. In other words, a shared delusion. Just take that in for a moment. Not only is truth based on nothing more than a perception, but our shared reality is little more than a dream. This destroys the nature of shared thought itself and renders all of society's conventions redundant. It destroys the social contract and legitimises 'the wah', chaos and anarchy. This leads to...

'My truth is whatever I feel it to be and I must ignore those who put facts and reason in my way. For my perception is the Truth.' This is the world of the 'Paranoid Schizophrenic'!

It is difficult to argue with some postmodernists because they will challenge any and all definitions, for 'he who defines, holds the power'. Yet, words without agreed meaning become useless. It is like trying to have a conversation with a young child who has not grasped the shared meaning of words such as: Responsibility, Earned, Duty, Sacred, Patience, Mutuality and Decency. For these are values, held in the Parent ego state, passed down by elders to the next generation. Postmodernists challenge the worthiness of such values.

The world turned inside out

The Parent Ego state P_2 is the part of our personality that would ordinarily stand up in opposition to such make-believe assertions. It retains our knowledge, history, values and culture. This is the ego state most often demonised by postmodernists. Even in Eric Berne's time, few Transactional Analysts saw real value in P_2. I was once asked by a participant on a TA course I was running: "Why do we need a Parent ego state?" The person had an anti-social aspect to his personality, so it was difficult for him to grasp my answer: "We need to know the difference between right and wrong, what behaviours are acceptable and to follow the golden rule as well as the law of the land. These shared values keep us civilised, otherwise what constrains us from annihilating one another? The Parent acts as the constraining force or brakes, acting in opposition to the desire or accelerator of the Child. A_2 simply chooses whether to accelerate or apply the brakes. It lacks the potency to stand up to the authoritarian impulse in C_2."

Contrary to what many believe, I believe P_2 is the most powerful part of our personality and one that we surrender at our peril. It is the part where we store all the real people we've met as well as our ancestors. It retains our family loyalties, cultural history, tribal affiliations, national pride, and sense of meaning and purpose. It is the most powerful part of us because it reminds us that 'it's NOT all about me'! Having confidence in our imperfect history propels us to want to become more evolved people. It's how we go about this that is the problem.

The postmodernists sought to demonise our parents, our institutions, our history and our values. One by one, they were deliberately targeted in the same way as God and Christianity had been undermined before. Led by titans such as Nietzsche, Feuerbach, Conte and Marx, they destroyed God and then Christianity.[41] In their wake, they led to a movement best described as 'Atheist Humanism,' a human-based creation, where we worship ourselves rather than a Transpersonal God. Paul Vitz in his excellent book 'Psychology as Religion: The Cult of Self-worship'[42], details how psychology and psychotherapy have been corrupted to arrive at this self-centred destination.

The dismantling of our institutions followed, as first the church, then law and order, journalism, politics, education, health, science and all institutions were re-invented. Postmodern thought was allowed to permeate our most treasured institutions as no one fought hard enough to save them. Playing on our doubts and fears, they demonised the

---

[41] (Henri de Lubac, 1944)
[42] (Paul Vitz, 1977)

West and its strongest players. In psychotherapy, Philip Larkin's poem 'This be the Verse' was much quoted:[43]

"They fuck you up, your mum and dad.
They may not mean to, but they do.
They fill you with the faults they had
And add some extra, just for you.

But they were fucked up in their turn
By fools in old-style hats and coats,
Who half the time were soppy-stern
And half at one another's throats.

Man hands on misery to man.
It deepens like a coastal shelf.
Get out as early as you can,
And don't have any kids yourself."

This poetry appealed to those who wished to blame others for their predicament. It's a grievance piece that seduced many millions in the West. Interestingly, not only did it demonise parents, it gave a not-so-subtle instruction in its last line. The fall in birth rate amongst the nations in the West fits in with such postmodernist thoughts. What better way of undermining Western thought than destroying the

---

[43] (Philip Larkin, 1971)

West from within by denying its next generation. Demographics alone show us that as we give up on having children, there will be fewer people to populate our nations. But the undermining of our values did not end there.

The 'Long March through the Institutions' was a term coined by Communist student activist Rudi Dutschke, a follower of Antonio Gramsci[44] and the Frankfurt School of Critical Theory.[45] It was a strategy for establishing the conditions for revolution: subverting society by infiltrating institutions such as the professions. Starting with our sources of knowledge, it worked its way into universities, schools and society. By infiltrating the institutions, it hollowed out our past, replacing it with new formulations that played on our doubts and fears; in Germany, it played on their war guilt; in the UK it shamed the nation because of our colonial past; in the USA it was racism and slavery that served to undermine national pride. Once made to feel guilty, ordinary people looked to the new religion for absolution. Only, unlike Christianity, postmodernism does not contain a redemption narrative. It keeps people in a subjugated position, afraid of saying and thinking the wrong thing. This is similar to what minority groups used to feel before they were liberated under the civil rights movements.

---

[44] (Antonio Gramsci, 2011)
[45] (Martin Jay, 1996)

The postmodern reformulation of 'civil rights' only applies to those that vote for the ideological left and are not politically in the centre or right-wing. What it amounts to is rights for some not for others – a return to the dynamics that existed pre-1960. That is why so many original civil rights leaders have called the postmodern reformulation a sham. Modern Human Rights movements only afford rights to the puritanical left and demonise all others...an illiberal reformulation of civil rights, posing as a liberal one.

Postmodernism challenges the assumptions that underlie our view of what reality is. It views the external world as less a self-evident truth and more a mass delusion that we all buy into. That we have socially constructed the world, its institutions and hierarchies, so as to oppress some people and exert power over them. Postmodern thought contends that the success of the West has been through enslaving and subjugating certain groups of people, and that 'White man' is the oppressor. Thus, 'Critical Theory'[46] blames 'power structures' and speaks to grievance culture.

In 1970, the American Feminist Carol Hanisch coined the phrase, "The personal is political" which captured many imaginations. It destroyed the sanctity of the private world of the individual by challenging our right to hold private views that oppress women. Later this was extended to other

---

[46] (Theodor Adorno & Max Horkheimer, 1973)

'minority' groups. It challenged our right to think our own thoughts! This assertion led to the PC movement that took upon itself the puritanical right to censor our thoughts. It turned our private world inside out and allowed politics to infiltrate all aspects of our lives. In TA terms, it is a Racket.

Those who feel aggrieved, or wish to help those who they believe are being disadvantaged by the 'system', readily take to this blame narrative. It is seductive because it appeals to the Child ego state. This narrative has only recently received significant pushback, yet has embedded itself in most Western nations. Taking the rules of the inner world, more weight is given to assertion than to fact; traditional knowledge or epistemology is discounted; subjective sentiment trumps objective truth. In other words, the world of the infant C_2 is given more importance than the world of the Adult A_2. This, I would contend, is no more than a Child's fantasy, masquerading as reality. Our world has been turned inside out as we now share a world based on imaginary, subjective perceptions and imaginary dangers; the real, objectivity we used to share as well as the real dangers we face, have now been forced into the private world of the individual. We have been first seduced then coerced into silence. The outer world of common sense has been replaced by the imaginings of a corrosive ideology; the inner world now contains the private thoughts we dare not make public, while the public world is one full of virtue signalling. How have we been so willing to accept this?

Groupthink

This psycho-political narrative is difficult to sell to free-thinking individuals. Yet, history tells us that crowds of people can be manipulated to believe fanatically. History is littered with accounts of massacres, insurrections and pogroms when people turn against their neighbours because their passions have been deliberately inflamed.

Both Adolf Hitler and Joseph Goebbels used the term *große Lüge* or 'Big Lie'. In Mein Kampf, Hitler wrote, "Here they were acting on the true principle that within a big lie, a certain fraction of it is always accepted and believed. At the bottom of their hearts, **the great masses of a people are more likely to be misled by their emotions than to be consciously and deliberately bad.** In the primitive simplicity of their minds, **they will more easily fall victim to a large lie than a small lie**, since they sometimes tell petty lies themselves, but would be ashamed to tell a lie that was too big. They would never consider telling a lie of such magnitude themselves, or knowing that it would require such impudence, they would not consider it possible for it to be told by others. Even after being enlightened and shown that the lie is a lie, they will continue to doubt and waver for a long time and will still believe there must be some truth behind it somewhere, and there must be some other explanation. For this reason, some part of the most bold and brazen lie is sure to stick. This is a fact that all the great liars and liars' societies in this world know only too well and use regularly."[47]

Here is the ultimate psychological-manipulation playbook. Hitler knew how to appeal to people's emotions, to tap into their prejudices. He knew how to tell big lies and get away with it. Unfortunately, this book was banned in modern Germany and has now been banned in the UK. Rather than learning from history and how the evil pair brainwashed a whole nation, we have been prevented from knowing this. Instead, the mainstream media are applying the 'Goebbelsian lie' principle, and we the people are being told 'big lies', which we swallow whole. We continue to be caught in the 'big lie' and often refuse to wake up!

Ending in July 1794 the Reign of Terror of the French Revolution[48] demonstrated a fanatical zeal, where people were executed for having the wrong privilege or attitude. The infantile beliefs that so impassioned the mob were stoked by those that had ambitions of power. The people were fed 'big lies', and 'were misled by their emotions'. The people in the crowd were 'not consciously or deliberately bad'. Once unleashed, however, mobs took on a life of their own and the mob rampage eventually took the lives of its

---

[47] (Adolf Hitler, 2010) – my emphasis in bold
[48] (Ian Davidson, 2016)

ringleaders. For once reason was eliminated, what could stand in the way of unfettered hatred? This same 'madness of crowds' has been seen time and again turning peaceful protests into violent riots, demonstrating the worst excesses of human behaviour, and instilling pure fear and panic into the hearts of law-abiding citizens.

All it takes is for a seed of perceived injustice to be introduced to the group. Often it is a big lie, as so exemplified by Hitler and Goebbels. Once it grows it turns a group into a crowd and before long a peaceful protest into mob violence. Deliberately inflaming the passions in a mob is what political activists specialise in. One of Eric Berne's neighbours in Carmel, California was the well-known political activist, Saul Alinsky. In his book 'Rules for Radicals'[49], Alinsky advocates a 'by any means necessary' approach to defeating his political enemies. This approach includes deception, violence and using psychological techniques to manipulate the populace. It is interesting that he considers 'Lucifer' as the first radical and clearly believes that the radical has moral superiority to those that he sets out to defeat. This amounts to moral superiority being conferred by a man who considers Lucifer a radical like himself – akin to Mussolini praising Hitler. For him 'the end justifies the means', a 'Machiavellian' stance on life and one that real justice will not countenance. Originally Alinsky's

---

[49] (Saul Alinsky, 1989)

influence was limited to left-wing fringe groups. However, both under President Obama and Presidential candidate Hillary Clinton, his influence led to groups such as BLM and Antifa. Given the 'no holds barred' attitude advocated, perhaps this explains why the Democratic Party in the USA has veered so far to the left, adopting desperate measures since the 2016 presidential election.

Psychological warfare is what this is about and political activists have been trained in how to manipulate groups. Hitler and Goebbels had the playbook. The psychological crowd manipulation has been written about countless times in history. It explains how the Bolshevik revolution in the former USSR went off track. Lenin's natural successor, Leon Trotsky, was maligned by Josef Stalin. So much so, that Trotsky was pelted with rotten potatoes by a mob organised by Stalin's secret police. Thus, the revolutionaries turned against each other and Trotsky's fate was sealed. Stalin had the psychological upper hand, using mob rule to his advantage and to get rid of his political opponent.

The psychological concept of 'Groupthink' was put forward by Yale Professor of Psychology, Irving Janis[50], to explain why people can behave so differently in large groups. Janis postulates that sometimes in groups, individual people tend to set aside their own thinking in favour of the 'group belief'.

---
[50] (Irving Janis, 1982)

That is, some groups require members to believe certain things, without doubt, or scepticism. Such fanatical belief is something we have attributed to traditional, religious groups in the past. However, we are now encountering the same fervour and 'religious zeal' in groups that profess to be non-religious or even anti-religious.

The belief itself is not the real problem. After all, children often adopt beliefs that they later update or even discard. Rather, **it is how the belief is believed** that reveals the 'rules of groupthink'.

Rule One is that the belief is more to do with **fantasy and make-belief** than with objectively verifiable facts. Postmodernists such as Foucault have asserted subjective (Child) beliefs as their preferred 'reality' and would dismiss the mature Adult ego state altogether. Thus, Rule one promotes dogmatic rather than rational beliefs.

Rule Two states that believers are **'morally superior'** in some ways to non-believers or 'deniers'. This is the danger I referred to earlier in these modern-day puritans. The advantage of believing is that it places believers in a self-satisfied and arrogant position relative to less modern outlooks.

The Third rule is that **dissident thoughts cannot be tolerated** and debate not entered into. Anyone that does not subscribe to the groupthink must be considered unintelligent or a denier.

Such beliefs are really dogma, expressed fervently, maintained passionately and defended forcefully. There is no room then for either a mature Adult or mature Parent ego state in such a crowd. No scepticism or wisdom. Thus, there is no room for individual thought, only a hive mind.

The global issues of our time

The same groupthink phenomena can be applied to many of the 'right-minded' issues of our times, where 'science' is often quoted as the final arbiter in public disagreements. My final dissertation at university was on the Philosophy of Science and the two different viewpoints on 'what science is' being advanced by Karl Popper [51] and Thomas Kuhn[52]. Popper's viewpoint was based on fact, logic and reason, whereas Thomas Kuhn believed that scientific advances were down to psychological crises that led to paradigm shifts. The former believed that science was never 'settled' because it was always open to falsification or revision. Kuhn's vision was a modern reformulation that highlighted the 'human' aspect or emotions behind the adoption of scientific theories. Kuhn's version described what science was becoming, rather than what it had traditionally stood for. In that way, Kuhn's vision paved the way for postmodern reformulations of science. Since, if emotion played such a big part in deciding what was scientifically sound, surely it was susceptible to influence from money and politics? Governments could use science just as they had used religion in the past. To maintain a firm grip on the unsuspecting populace.

---

[51] (Karl Popper, 1959)
[52] (Thomas Kuhn, 1962)

For instance, as a scientist, I have remained sceptical and curious about Al Gore's assertion that carbon dioxide was a greenhouse gas that could create a thermal blanket that led to global warming.[53] Having studied this possibility while at university, I knew there were differences of scientific opinion on climate change, with some scientists predicting global freezing and the coming of the next ice age.

My scepticism was raised when I became aware of how little actual evidence there was, yet so much public acclaim for the theory. So much so that real scientists were being drowned out behind a chorus of celebrity scientists and ordinary people who were acting from panic[54]. Psychology was being used to induce fear and produce a groupthink panic. Fear was being pumped into ordinary people and the term 'settled science' appeared as people feared a mass casualty event. Remember the same trick over 'Weapons of Mass Destruction' that led to the war in Iraq? Once public sentiment is marshalled by a corrupt regime, it overpowers reason, logic and facts. That is groupthink in action.

Is it possible that reason has given way to emotion? That what we are witnessing is a hoax being propagated on the general public, and that the goodness in people is being exploited for political ends? It was widely reported that a

---

[53] (Gregory Wrightstone, 2017)
[54] (Dr Patrick Moore, 2021)

co-chair of the UN Intergovernmental Panel on Climate Change recently revealed the real reason for pursuing a policy on climate change: "We redistribute de facto the world's wealth by climate policy," said Edenhofer. "One has to free oneself from the illusion that international climate policy is environmental policy. This has almost nothing to do with the environmental policy anymore." This all begins to sound like Marxism in disguise. The fact that this quote is so disputed online, shows that there is no single opinion on global warming, only two sides fighting it out. There is no 'Settled Science'.

Postmodern ideology thrives on asserting a big lie that sounds possible. It relies on manipulating public sentiment rather than private individual feelings. Remember the playbook master saying " **the great masses of a people are more likely to be misled by their emotions than to be consciously and deliberately bad.**" People were being told that we had only a short time to save the planet from anthropogenic climate warming brought about by carbon dioxide.[55] Whilst there is general agreement that the temperature of the earth is slowly increasing, there is no 'settled science' on the subject. The term 'settled science' is more a religious phrase than a scientific one; science can never be settled because of its very nature. It has always been a search for truth based on theories or hypotheses

---

[55] (Rex Fleming, 2020)

that require evidence to back them and this evidence may contradict or support a hypothesis. Science originally stood against religious dogma and religious fervour. It now appears that this fight may have been lost. There is too much money and politics riding on science for it to remain true to its original mission. It has become riddled with groupthink and has lost its appeal as a subject that could be trusted by all. Much of modern science has been corrupted and has lost the same innocence of truth that once we attributed to the free press – before it morphed into the mainstream media and became the province of wealthy owners and the plutocracy.

'Settled or Establishment Science' has become a political tool, used as a means of maintaining the groupthink, with alternative scientific opinions being quashed or ignored.

Al Gore's assertion and subsequent predictions have not materialised. It is now no longer called global warming, but climate change. It may be a 'big lie', used to mislead the general public and create an atmosphere of fear and panic. While the fanatics may call me a 'climate denier', I need more than computer models and graphs to convince me of the misconceived claims. I look at ice core data and actual measurements and hold Karl Popper's view that real scientific theories need to be 'falsifiable' and reproducible. An assertion is not proof; it is simply a hypothesis, no matter how many people get behind it. Shouting is not evidence, but simply reveals a passion and a felt sense of how things should behave. It's another racket.

Illiberal reformers

So embedded has postmodernism become, that we are now living through times where we can be prevented from expressing certain beliefs, opinions and from holding certain attitudes. In the UK, Harry Miller was investigated by the police who wanted to 'check his thinking', in an Orwellian style of authoritarianism.[56] The 'thought police' were acting on the concept of 'hate speech', yet were not limiting their investigation to what he said, but intruding into his head! We can nowadays be cancelled, de-platformed, demonetised, demonised, and so have our livelihoods and lives threatened, simply for having 'the wrong opinion'. So, whilst Modernism gave rise to Liberal Humanism, **Postmodernism has birthed an illiberal humanist movement, one that uses authoritarian means to hold onto power.**

Traditionally, Humanism was linked to liberalism. Nowadays, however, there is disagreement among humanists. Yuval Harari divides Humanism into 3 types.[57] Writing in 2015, he considers the largest group to be the Individual Humanists (or the classic liberals, to which a lot of TA therapists have some affinity). They believe that humanity is Individualistic and liberal. Then there are

---
[56] (The Times, 2020)
[57] (Yuval Harari, 2015)

Collective or Socialist Humanists, who believe that humanity is collective and finds true expression in groups. Lastly, he calls the third group the Evolutionary or Progressive Humanists, who believe that "Humans might degenerate into subhumans or evolve into superhumans." They believe that some people are 'morally superior' to others.

What we are nowadays witnessing in the West is infighting amongst humanists for a definition of what constitutes 'humanity'. Postmodernism has forged an intersectional coalition (the enemy of my enemy is my friend), of the 'collective' and the 'evolutionary' humanists; the 'collective' with its expertise in mobilising the 'mob,' and the 'evolutionary' humanists who implant the idea of 'moral superiority'. This is a dangerous collaboration, since they seek, more than anything, to bring down individualism and classic liberalism, which they both see as their enemy. Intersectional humanism has sometimes been called 'Neo-Liberalism' to disguise its original, illiberal roots.

Intersectional Humanism, then is a religion, albeit a secular one. This version, born from postmodernism, now worships the collective and evolution rather than respecting the individual. The danger is that by becoming puritanical, this strand of humanism has become authoritarian instead of liberal. The scars of the two world wars fought in Europe in the last century testify to illiberal ideologies that once were hailed and later condemned.

Both 'collective' and 'evolutionary' humanism may promote a desire to do good by engaging in group projects. This is what attracts so many followers. Yet, both believe in an orthodoxy of political opinion and have pushed aside Voltaire's defence of Freedom of Speech[58], as well as the First Amendment of the American Constitution. For freedom of speech is closely allied to freedom of thought. If one cannot share one's thoughts, there is no room for alternative formulations, and society regresses to the times of Galileo's trial[59] in the face of the powerful Roman Catholic Church. Under the duress of being faced by coercive power, such as a mob baying for blood, it is a well-known fact that people may buckle under intense pressure and can betray everything and everyone they once held dear.

The fact is that brainwashing works particularly well on well-intentioned, intelligent people, who want to do good in the world. Their rich inner world allows them to imagine – and it is this imagination that is being manipulated by psychological means; political activists employ mind control techniques. People in groups are particularly susceptible, as

---
[58] (Evelyn Beatrice Hall, 1906)
[59] (Richard Blackwell, 2008)

a mixture of fear and passion grips each individual, and the crowd takes on a life and often violence of its own.

When many of us think of aggression or violence, we usually only consider the physical form, most often attributed to men. There is, however, a psychological form of violence more often attributed to women – Reputation Destruction. This often involves engaging in malicious gossip, spreading lies, shunning, turning a group against a certain member and making them the pariah or scapegoat. This psychological form of coercion is nowadays most often found on social media and can result in people being ousted from their social groups or even from their jobs. Both forms of violence serve the same cause – Coercion or 'Shut Up and Obey', the instruction given to the slave.

Violence is an attempt to force or coerce another human being to do one's bidding. In our present times, it is psychological violence or reputation destruction that is most prevalent, as seen in Ad hominem attacks, cancel culture, BDS movements, and reporting someone to the police under the guise of 'Hate Speech'.

Social rules have been reformulated to rely less on reason and more on emotion. There is no need for evidence, only assertion. Thus mass hysteria is being allowed to dominate our society and authoritarian attitudes are all too common.

WOKE v AWAKE

We are finding the modern world deranged because the subjective, emotional experience of the inner world has been replacing the objective, rational reality of the traditional outer world. This over-emotional rhetoric has been the dominant narrative on both social media and mainstream media. However, 2016 revealed another narrative that has been developing and growing within Western nations. This has been called many things, including 'Populism', 'Nationalism', 'Common Sense' and is seen by left-wing ideologues as 'Alt-Right' or 'Extreme Right-Wing'. This terminology attempts to define the obvious split in cultural opinion now evident in society.

Many young people have given their own names to this phenomenon. The WOKE movement may have emerged originally from the traditional left, but is now not only about economics. It is no longer 'classic liberal' but has morphed into an intersectional movement, one that promotes the politics of 'Identity', 'Political Correctness' and 'Social Justice'. Those identifying as WOKE consider that the outer world needs to change to reflect their inner world. **They see the problems, not as ones that originate within themselves, but ones that are caused by the unjust world they see around them.** Their only solution is to tear down these structures (often old statues) instead of reforming the institutions that they already largely dominate. Blame is therefore not only considered a justifiable approach, but it is the only weapon in their armoury. If they can convince the populace that some people did bad things to them, then there may be reparations. Their stance does not however contain a redemption narrative. What happens next?

The other group is growing fast. They think of themselves as AWAKE, they are usually conservative or classic-liberal in nature, and have come to realise that they have been deceived by a lie from the political left. For them, the promise of the world after the Civil Rights push of the 1960s has not materialised. Considering themselves as 'hoodwinked', they have now 'taken the red pill' (a reference to the film, 'The Matrix'), and are aware of the forces at work in the public world that is keeping the WOKE collective under a spell. They see little but lies and deception from the political left; that Democrat-run cities have failed to deliver their promise to blacks and other minority groups. They consider that the 'blame narrative' from the intersectional lobby encourages a 'victim' mentality and no aspiration, only unrealistic expectations of free handouts. Black intellectuals like Carol Swain[60] and Thomas Sowell[61], have added their voice to this viewpoint since victimhood only promotes a view that blacks must

---

[60] (Carol Swain, 2002)
[61] (Thomas Sowell, 2013, 2019)

depend on the whites, and this is condescending. Furthermore, it denies personal Agency' by not requiring minorities to act directly on their own behalf.

As our opposing world views collide, we have a psychological split evident in our Western society, and a real danger that our irreconcilable differences may lead to civil unrest and possibly a civil war. Alternatively, in accordance with what is often misattributed to Hegel[62], that the opposing 'thesis' and 'antithesis' will result in a new 'synthesis'. Psychologically, we are being turned inside out. As the two systems clash for primacy, we have the clash of civilisations, cultures and the madness of our times.

Why does all this matter? Surely, we have always disagreed and yet found a way through this? And, so we might... but at what cost, and what might other nations make of the Western world tearing itself apart in this way? Are there not other nations that might wish for the whole liberal project to fail? **This is called Liberticide, the destroyer of liberty.** What awaits in the wings once we have navel-gazed ourselves into irrelevance?

---

[62] (Gustav Mueller, 1958)

Two distinct narratives

A narrative is a way of thinking, a way of interpreting, a way of experiencing, a way of believing and a way of becoming. In essence, it provides meaning to our lives. For instance, if you believe that someone is being treated cruelly, you may identify with them and see them as a 'victim' (note lower case v). You may wish to protect them, even fight on their behalf. On social media, you may be celebrated for your right-mindedness and get lots of approving 'likes' (strokes). If you engage a lot in this type of encounter, you may soon emerge as an SJW (Social Justice Warrior). A lot of people may follow you and you start to lead a movement. To keep your stroke balance full, you will need to find new 'victims' to write about. There are plenty out there who self-identify as the 'victim' and more do-gooders like you that swoop in to defend them. 'Outrage' becomes your identity and hatred of what you consider cruel defines you. Political attitude soon takes over, and you no longer care so much about cruel acts, but more about whether a person has the right political attitude. If the person who was stabbed is 'on your side' you hate on the stabber, but if the stabber is the one on your side... you give them a free pass and ignore the person who was stabbed – they probably deserved it anyway for being a racist/ sexist/ homophobe/ transphobe. And so, this narrative goes. It has become a religion which defends its members, for 'my truth is whatever I feel it to be and I must ignore those who put facts and reason in my way... for they are the enemy!'

Now, look at the same situation through the lens of traditional TA. In a Game, a 'Victim' is not 'innocent'. Instead, they play an invisible-yet-vital part in proceedings. Victims contribute to their predicament. **Victims are viewed as those with masochistic urges,** not as some poor person who deserves pity.

Secondly, a Rescuer intervenes not out of necessity, but out of a felt need to be the Victim's champion (note capital V and capital R). Remember that **the Rescuer in TA is stealing the other person's Agency** through being over-helpful. Stroking a person for playing a role in a Game simply keeps them stuck in their Script; a society-programmed version or slave.

The Progressive movement started in the USA in 1890. Originally, it was an Evangelical movement that wanted to do good in the world. "The protest of the progressives originated not out of personal suffering but rather out of moral and intellectual discontent with the suffering (and enrichment) of others."[63] This 'do-gooder' attitude had a superiority complex at its heart, (I+U-), as found in most religions. Later the movement became more associated with secular preferences, yet retained its religious zeal. "The

---

[63] (Thomas C Leonard, 2020)

progressives' urge to reform America sprang from an evangelical compulsion to set the world to rights, and they unabashedly described their purposes as a Christian mission to build a Kingdom of Heaven on earth."[64] This then was the narrative that persuaded many 'right-minded' people to adopt a 'victimhood' mentality. The Rescuers needed a supply of 'victims' to continue their mission.

In TA the Victim is not doing the self-identifying. They are not 'innocent'. Just because someone believes they are the Victim is insufficient. Assertion with no evidence is simply not enough. Go into any prison, anywhere, and ask the inmates whether they are guilty? Their universal conviction that they are innocent is at odds with society finding them guilty. Society, through a court process involving laws, a judge, two competing advocates and a jury of 12 peers, makes that judgement… and the person was regarded as innocent until proven guilty, and was found guilty beyond reasonable doubt. These legal processes attempt to maintain the confidence of the public, by emphasising Human Rights, Fairness and above all, Justice. Whereas there are undoubtedly cases where those found guilty were wrongly tried, the system has been largely successful and is much better than what it replaced… trial by the mob, a witch trial, followed by a lynching, drowning or hanging! This is the narrative into which TA was born. It condemned

---

[64] (Thomas C Leonard, 2020)

those who held themselves up to be Judge, Jury and Executioner. It abhorred slavery and injustice. It believed in 'innocent until found guilty', a legal process. It considered an assertion as nothing more than that, and certainly not in lieu of fact. Thus, Berne's concept of the Adult Ego State had reason, truth and knowledge central to it. There was no room for Foucault's belief system other than as Child fantasy contaminating the Adult.

Going back to the first narrative, an SJW will believe that their 'victim' is innocent and apply social media rules. Social media has 'pity' as its judge, a concept made popular by Jean-Jacques Rousseau.[65] Yet, pity is born of a 'superior' moral stance, an I+U- attitude. It has more to do with religion than justice. For if I pity the person who just stabbed someone and then asserts he was provoked into doing it, what about the real Victim who is bleeding? What about if the person carrying out the stabbing, says he was righteous and carried out the violent act because the other person had the 'wrong political belief'? That the other person was a 'deplorable'? In a court of law, this does not amount to a valid defence. What about on social media? Defences that would be inadmissible in a court of law are often used in the court of public opinion.

---

[65] (Jean-Jacques Rousseau, 1762)

This battle of opposing narratives occurs whenever there is more weight given to assertion than to fact, when knowledge or epistemology is discounted and when subjective sentiment trumps objective truth. In other words, when the world of infant assertion is given more importance than the world of the evidence-seeking Adult... cue the Kavanaugh trials 2018, where there were many accusations made but very little admissible evidence presented. The 'ME TOO' movement emerged more from mass hysteria than principled reason. Many considered the Kavanaugh hearing a 'witch trial', where assertion led to calls of 'Believe Her'.

Care and Fairness

At the heart of the two-narratives divide lies a different attitude towards the concept of 'Care' (or LOVE) and 'Fairness' (or JUSTICE). One attitude is an unconditional formulation, the other a conditional one tethered to a requirement. We shall explore these here:

Do you believe that there is something called UNCONDITIONAL Love? That love places no conditions whatsoever on the involved parties? That love is like being in our mother's womb where no demands are made on us? Is it true that 'love is all you need?' The fact that so many loving relationships go wrong puts a dent in this notion. What happens to love in cases of infidelity or domestic abuse? Is unconditional love really no more than an infatuation?

Cared for ◄─────────── Caregiver

If you still believe in no conditions, does everyone deserve Unconditional love, to be looked after as a Fundamental Right? Is it an entitlement or is it earned or deserved? For instance, does the care constitute a demand needing to be met, or does the caregiver also have a say? Does this care involve an appreciation or love in return? Is it more like theft or freely given at no cost by the caregiver? Is caregiving an act of voluntary kindness, or a mandated order? Does the caregiver also have a right to be looked after and loved, and if so, by whom?

Cared for ⬅️ ➡️ Caregiver

This second diagram indicates that **care involves reciprocity**. Namely, that there needs to be something given to the caregiver by the Cared for. That is an appreciation or mutual love. This could be a positive stroke, such as thank you or a payment made in lieu. Whatever it is, it results in more care, not less. Where the bond is love, there is love on both sides. However, when the bond is guilt or financial reward, mutual appreciation is compromised. Because both parties have feelings, love is not the only thing in play.

The situation becomes even more complicated when an external agency is involved.

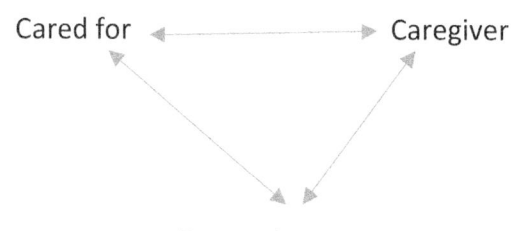

Cared for ⬅️ ➡️ Caregiver
         ↘   ↙
      External Agency

This more sophisticated diagram shows that reciprocity cannot be excluded. **For, unlike robots, humans have feelings**. A Cared for patient that does not treat the caregiver with decency and respect may not attract the best caregiving. Likewise, if the caregiver is given insufficient acknowledgement or reward by the external agency, this demoralises them. Similarly, if the funding of the external agency is too costly or insufficient funds are made available, the care quality is compromised. Also, if the caregivers act improperly towards their charges or become 'uncaring' in their attitude towards those they are meant to care for, there is a problem.

Because of so many complicating factors, Care has become an industry. The initial two-party contract became a three-party one by the involvement of insurance companies (whether private or state). However, to address Care Quality for the cared for, the welfare of carers and financial matters, several additional bodies end up being brought in. This can be the Care Quality Commission, Unions, Financial bodies, Arbitration bodies, legal bodies etc.

The child-like C$_2$ view does not contain all the complicating dynamics and simply wishes to eliminate their consideration. In simple terms, Care ought to be simple. Unfortunately, human nature is anything but simple and competing needs and demands need to be addressed. Contrary to the song, "Love is **not** all you need". You need Justice as well.

Fairness or Justice is another concept that requires exploration. In a child-like world, it is simply an act of distribution. Like taking a cake and dividing it amongst people. However, is it done according to the rules of Equality or those of Equity? Who decides? Are some people considered exempt from consideration, and if so how? Who decides who is entitled to cake and who is not? Is this done robotically or humanely? The latter once again involves human feelings. For instance, some people have more friends than others, some people are viewed as disadvantaged. Some people have more advocates or know how to market themselves better than others. Some people are better at exploiting their situation, at making a case for 'pity', while some genuinely vulnerable people suffer in silence without anyone standing up for them. Are some more entitled or more deserving than others? All these complex dynamics complicate the initial child-like picture.

In the child-like world, there are no shortages, no need to consider who baked the cake. However, in the real world, the cake did not bake itself. **Justice is tethered to consideration**.

Therefore, apart from the question of distribution, we need to consider the question of manufacture. Yet, in a child-like world, this is taken for granted. Whether the cake is made by an individual or a group of individuals, it still needs to be made. What motivates them to make such cakes? Is it appreciation, or an elevated status or a financial reward? Kindness can take you so far, but if you are not rewarded with something, human nature will kick in and your feelings will come to the fore. You might start out baking cakes for fun or take pleasure in your cakes being appreciated... but what next? What happens when you don't receive an appreciation or when someone doesn't like your cake? What about if they bang on your door demanding more? What about if someone abuses your cakes or abuses you? In short, the ideological view of a perfect world with you baking cakes for no reward and receiving an endless stream of purely positive support is a utopian dream. Human nature is a complex mix of often-competing desires and fears. **Resentment is based on a perceived lack of justice; a powerful emotion that can overpower love and often destroys relationships.** We need justice as well as love. We forget that at our peril.

The First Order Structural Ego State Model

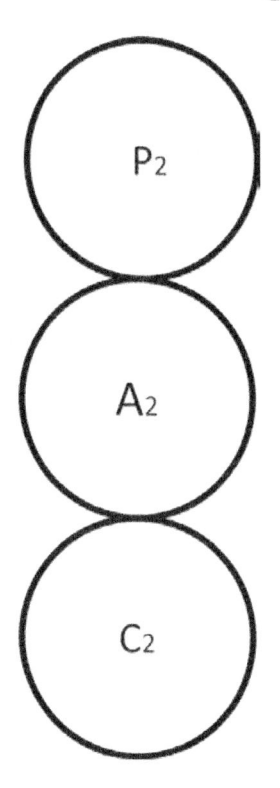

P_2

A_2

C_2

The internal world of each individual was described by Berne in his Structural Model of ego states. He also described how an individual can shift from one ego state to another, and may or may not be aware of when he does so. The shift may or may not be noticeable to the outside observer. Such a shift may occur consciously or unconsciously, through an act of will or a slip from one state to another.

Each ego state has its own, often different, set of attitudes, beliefs, thoughts and feelings associated with it. A person can have an I+U+ attitude in their P, while secretly being resentful or I+U- in their Child. When that person is in P, they may believe in peace and harmony for all humanity. Yet, coming across someone with whom they disagree politically, they enter C, resentment takes hold and they hate the other person. That is what TA theory tells us.

Before we go into a bit more detail, let's return to the structural model of ego states introduced in Part Two. The Child ego-state C_2 is the first to develop and is called the Archaeopsyche. This is a personal, subjective take on the world, where our wants and needs are paramount. As we reach the milestone when we can appreciate logic and reason, we begin to develop an Adult ego state A_2 or Neopsyche. This is a more objective and reasonable way of making sense. All the time, we have been taking in the rest of the world around us. We begin to realise that other people have their own needs, desires and sensitivities and that those might be different from our own. All the people who have influenced us get stored here. Elders play an important part in this, the most-mature part of us. This development is the beginning of the Parent ego state P_2 or Exteropsyche.

Therefore, a healthy, balanced individual has a set of ego states that look like this. The PAC labels have a number 2 beside them, to indicate that they are the most mature, developed states and the aim of TA psychotherapy is to arrive at this destination.

The tripartite model balances the experience of the self with that of the experiences of others. It is, thus, not an egocentric or a narcissistic view of personality. The Adult A_2 often acts as a mediator, between C_2 and P_2; it also acts as a place where free thought can occur. It allows for conflicting thoughts, reflection and contemplation. A mature A_2 responds rather than reacts. It does not allow feelings to overwhelm it, nor prejudice.

Postmodernists only really account for the Child (C_2) experience, so are at variance with the full 3 ego state make-up of the individual. They prefer the Second Order Model to the First.

The Second Order Structural Ego State Model

The PAC structure reveals some interesting details when it is looked at more closely. Each ego state is subdivided as shown below. Developmentally, the Archaeopsyche C_2 develops first, then the Neopsyche A_2 and finally the Exteropsyche P_2.

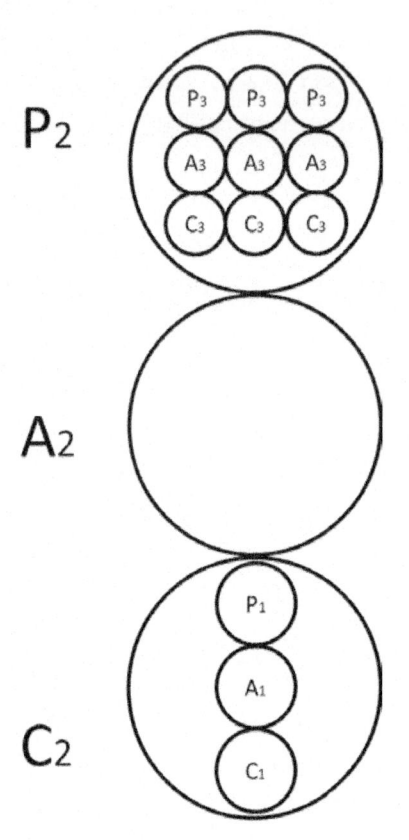

P_2 — contains $P_3, P_3, P_3, A_3, A_3, A_3, C_3, C_3, C_3$

A_2

C_2 — contains P_1, A_1, C_1

P_2 consists of all the people who have influenced our development, each with their own PAC structure, called P_3, A_3 and C_3. Some are more influential than others. P_2 acts as a database and source of wisdom, knowledge and history. It includes sources of culture, identity, religion and science.

A_2 is not subdivided since it consists of the here-and-now. It is the best place with which to process information and involves asking questions, using reason and knowledge to process information and making thought-out decisions. It responds rather than reacts and remains objective. It has access to P_2 as well as C_2 and mediates between the two.

C_2 consists of three primitive structures, all based on personal and subjective takes on the world. These may be thought of as early precursors or primitive versions of the fully developed version. P_1 is the primitive Parent or electrode or SPOOKY. A_1 is the primitive Adult or 'Little Professor' or SPUNKY. C_1 is the primitive Child or Somatic Child or SLEEPY. Unlike the mature 2s, the 1s rely on magical perceptions, intuition and instinct.

Berne had various names for P_1, such as the 'pig parent' or the 'electrode'. P_1 is the authoritarian impulse in us, the dictator and ruler of A_1 and C_1. It is the part of us that keeps us stuck in Child, and it's the part of us that holds the programme or script. P_1 often is rigid, exhibits black or white thinking and is susceptible to religious indoctrination. P_1 can be affected by brainwashing, as in the case when someone else's P_1 takes over. P_1 distorts the experience of the original caregiver. This distortion can both diminish or exaggerate the original experience so that P_1 can 'spook' by its power to deny or to terrify when it kicks in. P_1 was given the name of 'Spooky' by Fanita English[66], who viewed it as a survival-type parent, one often putting survival and not compassion as its primary focus. It acts to keep all other parts of the Child ego state in C_2 in line, like a drill sergeant. It can also ignore and see no danger or deny responsibility by blaming others. P_1 must be held in check by a combination of A_2 and P_2; otherwise, it will function to maintain the client in script. Postmodern ideology gives P_1 free rein by removing these more mature 'regulators'.

The world of the C_2 Child is rich in imagination, passion and creativity. Given the opportunity to develop and mature in an education system that believes in a plurality of ideas and tolerance for opposing views, it will flourish. However, if the Child is indoctrinated by political ideologies, it will not fully grow up and remain dependent for its stroke nourishment.

A_1 is different from A_2 in that the latter has access to all the ego states and can therefore act fully in the here-and-now. A_2 listens to the elders in P_2 as a source of wisdom and

---

[66](Fanita English, 1972)

knowledge, whereas A_1 limits itself to the 1s; consequently, it is often naïve, contemptuous and biased. It can become overwhelmed by emotion and accept indoctrination. A_1 is a child-version of the full Adult A_2 and comes to conclusions often intuitively, yet without sufficient logic, reason or facts. If selected to sit on a jury, for instance, a person using only A_1 will come to a decision without paying much attention to the facts. They will go by 'gut feel' rather than by evidence. Social media encourages A_1 and SJWs are prone to rushing to judgement by becoming outraged, revealing their bias, rather than appealing to a calm consideration.

C_1 is sometimes referred to as the 'body' or 'somatic' Child. When C_1 is active, the person is likely to experience pleasure or pain, often as comfort or distress (stress). C_1 causes discomfort through its release of anxiety. Anxiety can cause mild or severe symptoms, from nervousness to panic attacks to blindness or even paralysis. Anxiety often leads to individual symptoms. However, it can also lead to mass hysteria in crowds. It acts to make us manic, desperate and willing to do the unthinkable to reverse its debilitating effects; hence Groupthink is really mass hysteria.

In July 1518[67], in what came to be called 'the dancing plague', a dancing mania enveloped a group of people in Strasburg. Several hundred were struck by a sudden and

---

[67] (Erik Midelfort, 2000)

seemingly uncontrollable urge to dance. While many dancers collapsed from sheer exhaustion, some even died from strokes and heart attacks.

Interestingly, the same dancing plague broke out in many medieval cities in Europe. It initially left city elders at a loss to explain the bizarre phenomenon. However, it was eventually traced back to a superstitious belief attributed to St Vitus, who many believed could curse sinners to dance themselves to death. After two months, and many failed attempts to stop the dancers, the elders hit upon a solution. Since the belief was attributed to St Vitus, they transported the dancers to a mountain-top shrine to the saint where they could pray for absolution. In that way, their guilty consciences were freed of their sins and many regained functions of their limbs and stopped dancing. The episode of mass hysteria shows how guilt can take hold of a people's conscience and make them into hapless automatons.

It is something that is nowadays being deliberately exploited by those who prey on our guilt... only, in the absence of absolution, modern 'dancers' are likely to adopt a false belief that they are bad people - unless they dance to the tune of BLM, Antifa, Critical Theory, Green agendas and other beliefs being extolled by the ideological Left.

Back to postmodernism

Postmodernism has a seductive appeal to C_2 and its primitive, child-like internal structures P_1, A_1 and C_1. Since it has disavowed knowledge, facts and reason, it discounts the Adult A_2 and acts to dismiss the Parent P_2 ego state. Postmodernists value the feelings and subjective experience of the Child C_2 ego state over that of the thinking, objective experience of the full Adult A_2. They see only negative aspects in the Parent P_2 ego state, often demonising it and wishing to eliminate it altogether rather than reforming it. Thus, postmodernists only really recognise the one ego state, C_2, and therefore the primacy of P_1. Consequently, **the whole concept of First Order Ego States becomes redundant.**

At best, the only part ego states they will consider are P_1, A_1 and C_1. These are infantile versions and pose dangers, akin to allowing children to take charge of the police or the courts or politics and governance. Some extreme political ideologies are founded on such idealistic and non-realistic visions. **TA theory only really works as long as A_2 and P_2 are fully included.** Otherwise, the Child is made master and slave simultaneously. The Child is master because he is left unchallenged by contradictory and opposing viewpoints in P_2, and shielded from searching questions in A_2. The concept of a 'Safe Space' in American Universities[68] does precisely that. It is also a well-known tool used to reprogramme individuals who have the wrong political attitude, in authoritarian countries. However, the Child is also made a slave to those that tell him how and what to think, such as in 'Unconscious Bias Training'[69]; 'how' via an exogenous, imported A_1, and 'what' via a streamed-in P_1, that is more like an 'echo chamber' and less like a library. This is nothing short of political indoctrination masquerading as education; it aims to produce obedient clones rather than allow each person the freedom to become the person who they have the potential to be.

When postmodernists do acknowledge Parent, they are referring to P_1, not P_2. Yet calling it 'Parent' does not do it justice. They are referring to the internal, fantasy Parent, not to the real-life people in P_2. So, what's the difference and why is it important?

When I connect with my P_1, I hold many impulses that react to internal and external stimuli. For instance, becoming enraged by what I see as an act of injustice. I may even wish to punish the wrong-doer. If I am the 'wrong-doer' I may seek to punish myself. These are my fantasies, part-introjected from caregivers. Therapy has helped me to realise that there are better ways of speaking out on behalf

---

[68] (Teddy Amenabar, The Washington Post, 2016)
[69] (Sarah Fiarman, 2016)

of injustices and of helping us all see common sense. The danger of P_1 is that it does not consider anything outside of its 'sight zone'. It is a Child's take, after all.

When I connect with my P_2 however, I imagine myself convening a panel of experts that I respect, and whose values and expertise I can appreciate. This panel will have dissenting views and I appreciate the different voices. There will be a plurality of thought built-in and not a political orthodoxy. It will not resemble an 'echo-chamber'. In order to be effective, society has to have elders. For, as Jordan Peterson says in his book '12 Rules for Life'[70], you need to learn how to tidy up your own bedroom before you aspire to tidy up the world!

P_2 is not a concept that postmodernists can easily grab or accept. Their worldview will not see any positive in P_2, since they view it as a way of subjugating people, and the source of all the world's ills. They view P_2 as something that has to be eliminated. Hence, they 'throw out the baby with the bathwater'. This relates to their idealistic view of human nature and the left-wing ideologies that underpin postmodernism. They would often prefer to set everything on fire than to engage in more modest reform.

Likewise, Postmodernists do not appreciate A_2. The subjective A_1 reality is all they will really believe. Thus, if a

---

[70] (Jordan Peterson, 2018)

person's intuition tells them one thing, yet their logic and reason tells them something different, they will most often ignore A_2 and side with A_1. Consequently, without a full A_2, they are prone to rushing to judgement and subject to being accused of having double standards... and they do, for they don't really believe in standards after all. They are often 'Relativists' about most things, and resort to their misconception of Hegel's 'dialectic' as a way of explaining away their thought inconsistencies. "So, how can you square your belief in pacifism, with you beating someone with a baseball bat?" "How can you advocate for climate change, whilst taking private jets to attend an environmental conference?" A_2 fails them in such circumstances, so they have to resort to their passion and profess moral superiority in their A_1 and P_1 instead.

So, does a crowd not have an A_2 or P_2? In short, NO. Crowd manipulators are the ones trained in how to indoctrinate and dominate the mob. They have learned how to use slogans, chants and other techniques, perfected in cults and authoritarian movements. These appeal directly to P_1. Saul Alinsky learned his craft by working with the mafia mobs in Chicago after all. They taught him how to use fear to manipulate the masses, to engage in mind control, much like the mafia did with shopkeepers during the Prohibition era.

Projective Identification

Mind control can best be understood by reference to 'Projective Identification', a term introduced by Melanie Klein, whereby in a close relationship, as between a mother and child, lovers, or therapist and patient, "parts of the self and internal objects are split off and projected into the external object, which then becomes possessed by, controlled and identified with the projected parts."[71] In R.D. Laing's words, "The one person does not use the other merely as a hook to hang projections on. He/she strives to find in the other, or to induce the other to become, the very embodiment of projection."[72] **This is projecting INTO not ONTO**.

In psychotherapy, the therapist is meant to 'adequately process' their own responses or 'countertransference' to these intense projections coming from the client. Successful therapy will therefore entail the therapist experiencing these projections and staying alert to the fact that they are revealing something about the client's state of mind. If the therapist takes them personally, the therapy is compromised. The therapist needs to remember that the projections are revealing the private world of their client, rather than exposing something about the therapist.

---

[71] (Hanna Seagal, 1964)
[72] (Ronald David Laing, 1969)

However, sometimes the projections are so strong or the identification is so intense, that the client will continue to believe that any response from the therapist 'proves' that they were coming from the therapist all along!

In therapy, these are unconscious processes. However, the same Projective Identification processes can be used consciously. In other words, they can be taught and they can be learned. Just as in the way that the charm and easy manner of a genuine car salesman, can be taught to people who lack that natural capacity.

Projective Identification is a special form of Projection that involves much more emotional force so that it gets past the other person's psychological defences. The other person lowers their guard either under the spell of seduction, or by consent as with a therapist, or under the threat of coercion as in a group that demands compliance.

This means that under special conditions, such as under extreme duress, people can be programmed. One of the central tenets of TA is that **Everyone has the capacity to think for themselves,** except for the severely brain-damaged. We cannot be MADE to feel or behave in particular ways by others, or by our surroundings. 'We are responsible for our own feelings and behaviour.' **However, under duress or in a trance state, we can be induced to take on another person's will.** Likewise, we can think very differently if we are afraid and have adapted to the norms of a group or a cult. Real thinking involves being individuated and not being the mouthpiece of an advantageous position, ideology or religion.

"(People)... under the influence of projective identification are characterised by coercion, manipulation, ensorcellment, intimidation, ridicule by imitative caricature, and martyrdom. Patients who feel that they are 'sleepwalking', 'possessed' or acting like 'zombies' and robots, are afflicted with projective identification."[73]

According to Grotstein, "Projective identification may be used as a type of defence, a means of communicating, a primitive form of relationship, or a route to psychological change; used for ridding the self of unwanted parts or for controlling the other's body and mind."[74]

Eric Berne did not fully develop his 'Energy Theory' which may have explained the mechanism behind Projective Identification and hypnosis. That is, in the space between people, an energy exchange is taking place as well as an exchange of information. The intention of each participant constitutes energy. It is real and present just like an ulterior.

---

[73] (James Grotstein, 1981)
[74] (James Grotstein, 1981)

In summary, then, Projective Identification is the forceful projection of one person's intention into that of another to achieve an element of control over the other. There are 2 categories of Projective identification.

The first is the more benign form called Empathy, where we scan the other person and are scanned by them. By tuning-in in this way, we aim to get a deeper understanding of each other's intents and motivations. It is like 'baring our souls' and can leave us feeling vulnerable as well as really heard. We can think of this as sharing the information in our personal diaries or bank accounts. **It's like 'scanning the joint'... sometimes as a prelude to committing a crime!**

It is arguably a more benign form of control because it is about making the other person more predictable. Akin to letting another person into your home. Contrary to popular belief, everyone is capable of 'empathy' but it is highly personal, and ethically it is an intrusion that should require consent. Nevertheless, it has been made popular and is a narcissistic tool to attempt to mind read someone else's intent. Many of us use sympathy or some form of compassion instead, since it doesn't require getting into the other person's head.

The second form of projective identification involves a transfer both into and from the other. That is an exchange of parts of the psyche. It is akin to a burglary where one person walks into the psyche of another, stealing their peace of mind and leaving behind an unwanted part of themselves. Thus, they simultaneously rid themselves of a 'bad' bit and steal a 'good' bit from the other. We can think of this as altering the entries in our personal diaries or bank accounts, to our detriment and to benefit the other. **It's like committing the crime!**

It is a malign form of control because it involves imposing one's will into another. This is done either through seduction or coercion. Akin to walking through an open doorway, stealing and planting an unwanted gift. So, how does this work? Can anyone do it?

To understand the complex dynamics of Projective Identification, it is important to realise that some people are better at it than others, since it requires 'potency' or a strong will to impose and a recipient who, being placed in a compromised position, is susceptible to the projection. It is best carried out at close quarters, with sufficient eye contact, and possibly touch. The setting may be an intimate one, or it can be done in a group. The important aspect is that it has to feel personal and that the only way to end it is via capitulation. The recipient's response must be to acquiesce. This then is the basis for brainwashing, a type of hypnosis.

> By calling you a bad name, I pass my badness into you...you racist, sexist, xenophobic...

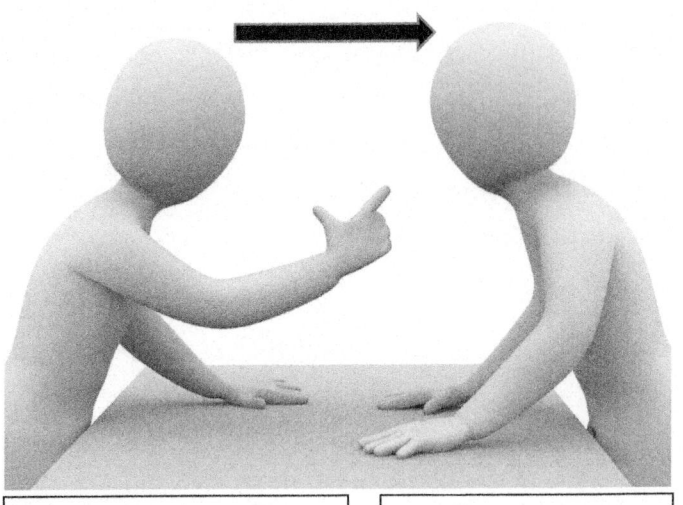

| I feel morally superior to you...now that I have forced my badness into you | I feel bad in being called out...maybe I'm a bad person and should feel guilty |

This is one way to impose one's will. The person on the left is shouting and threatening the one on the right. This could be a boss and an employee, or a cult leader calling the other a racist, homophobe, transphobe. The person on the right has to believe it and is under the spell. This is often referred to as transference and counter-transference. The projection has 'forced a response', that allows the accuser to continue to believe he was right to identify such a 'badness' in the first instance. Yet, this was really a case of 'what I see in thee, is really present in me.' – **I was the one who planted the wallet, that I then accused you of stealing!**

This is worse still if carried out in a group since the person is shamed into submission.

"Shame, shame, shame... You're either with us, or you're against us!"

Try it out by staring directly at someone at close quarters and getting them to do the same to you. See who blinks first! Establishing the dominance scenario is used by boxers before fights.

Projective Identification explains why so many of us get caught up in psychological games. Some people are more forceful projectors than others whereas some people are more insecure and prone to reacting to the forcefulness of the projector. Games are like spells. We need to be honest about just how forceful and controlling we are all capable of being and not just see ourselves as innocent Victims.

Mind control often manipulates our sense of Trust. Whereas Trust is a fundamental capacity that we are born with, many of us have been trained to trust authority figures or to distrust them. Many of us trust our relatives, friends and consensual reality. Some of us, however, seek out independent sources to check out which are trustworthy. Learning to trust ourselves as well as discerning who to trust, is a capacity we need to develop as we grow up.

To avoid being manipulated, we need to ask searching questions, engage with different opinions and have access to a variety of sources of information. Be aware that we are living through challenging times where powerful projectors such as the media, celebrities and moral doomsayers are trying to force us to their will – good or otherwise!

Cults

In cults, people are programmed via a variety of 'projective identification' techniques, akin to Ensorcellment or brainwashing. These often involve shouting, shunning, deprivation, love bombing, incarceration and many other inhumane techniques to 'break them'. This is all about submission and the ultimate threat is to oust them from the group so that they are then cut off from their sources of strokes – their 'new' friends and family. Cults know that the need to 'belong' is so fundamental to sentient humans, that some would rather starve and kill themselves than face the prospect of being alone and isolated. Often, as in gang culture, each person is required to carry out an 'initiation' act; one so egregious or 'deviant', such as betrayal or injurious behaviour, including torture, rape or even murder, that they cannot go back from it. This effectively severs the bond with their original family and their old friends. They then become dependent on their 'new friends' who they initially see as their unconditional friends. It is only later, when they start to experience unconscionable things, that they think about leaving. Only, by then it has become extremely difficult to leave because the cult members show their coercive side and fear of rejection has been instilled in anyone who wishes to break ranks. This psychological manipulation is well documented. What many have not yet realised, is that the size of the cult knows no limits.

Communist China, just like the USSR before it, perfected cult psychology. Leaders sought to keep the masses under control and enlisted the support of so-called 'journalists' to help paint a picture that kept the masses under an illusion or 'spell'. The so-called 'Free Press' was used to help indoctrinate the populace, and dissenters were removed without the press reporting on it. Concentration camps were used to keep these agitators from the main body of the often-compliant population. Similarly, Marxists maintained an unnatural culture, as seen in East Berlin before the fall of the wall. This has sometimes been referred to as 'Cultural Marxism', a term hated by the ideological left, for it exposes their deception.

How many of us, unwittingly, belong to large cults? If you fear being rejected by your friends or family simply for having a different opinion, then you may already be a cult member. The chat show host, Dave Rubin[75], describes his two most difficult decisions. When he came out as gay, having kept himself in the closet for 25 years, he was pleasantly surprised. Many on the political left embraced him and he felt he belonged, so he thought, unconditionally. Well, when he decided that he was a 'classic liberal' free thinker, rather than a 'Progressive' intersectional-tied thinker, his former friends not only disowned him but have persecuted him relentlessly for it. His belief in individual

---

[75] (Dave Rubin, 2020)

liberty came into stark contrast with those whose belief in the collective hive-mind, had made them anti-personal freedom, and therefore illiberal. So much for unconditional belonging. They felt as though they 'owned him' for being gay. Once he wasn't a 'progressive', they hated him. They thought he had betrayed them, but all it did was reveal their real agenda – Groupthink trumps free thought!

Cultural Marxism involves making people believe not just in the economic theory of Karl Marx. Instead, it turns Socialism into Communism, for it aims to defeat Individualism. Free thinking individuals threaten the political orthodoxy of Cultural Marxism. Vladimir Lenin was the first to use the term 'Political Correctness', insisting that people in the then USSR must have the correct political opinion. That made sense given his oppressive ideology. However, those who now promote political correctness, often fail to understand that they are using a concept made popular by the autocratic leader. It is not possible to promote PC, whilst simultaneously believing that they are 'good, free people'. Unless they really worship an Authoritarian rather than a Libertarian world.

The split world we inhabit

A 'psychological split' is an inability to simultaneously hold opposing thoughts, feelings or beliefs. A person who 'splits' sees the world in terms of black or white – all or nothing.

James Grotstein wrote 'Splitting and Projective Identification' in 1981[76]. The dust cover of the book makes a bold and prophetic statement: "In its first hundred years, psychoanalysis has been a history of the mechanism of REPRESSION and DISPLACEMENT. In its second hundred years, it will be a history of SPLITTING and PROJECTIVE IDENTIFICATION." Grotstein hits the nail on the head by describing splitting as an inability to talk across opposing narratives. This happens to some extent within all of us as individuals and is particularly found amongst those with antisocial, borderline or narcissistic personality issues.

Splitting is a psychological defence mechanism, found in individuals. It keeps the individual from knowing some truths that they find too difficult to process and reconcile. For instance, as in someone who has experienced trauma. In trauma, there are often two opposing processes; the **need to remember** battles it out with the **need to forget**. A split individual will not seek to balance these out. Instead, the 'split' involves adopting one stance and denying the other. This can mean an inability to stop reliving the trauma,

---

[76] (James Grotstein, 1981)

being plagued by recurring nightmares and flashbacks, feeling intense feelings and having intrusive thoughts. Alternatively, an individual may be on the amnesia side of the split, cut off from all memory, denying the reality of what happened, or how emotionally and cognitively different they now are. The split prevents healing and reaching a balanced sense of self; it's an altered personality, an internal struggle from which there is no harmony or mood stability.

Just as in individuals, splitting also occurs in groups. A split group is one that only acknowledges one side of a debate. Just as in the case of a split individual, a split group defies reality and lives in a type of delusion. Such groups have traditionally been found in religious cults, gangs and cliques. That is, in groups that are difficult to join and difficult to leave. What they have in common is their rigid dogma, their restrictive view of reality and their inability to engage in a meaningful, open exchange with anyone that does not share their views.

Political activists benefit from keeping us split. 'Divide and conquer' is a well-known means of exerting power over the populace. Whether or not we are divided into the 'haves' and the 'have-nots' or by 'group identity' such as men v women, blacks v whites or heterosexual v LGBTQ, it is still a means of using human differences to divide us for political purposes.

Psychological hatred of 'the other' is a tribal instinct; stoking that is behind much of the mind splitting. It is why splits persist even in the face of facts and reason. The splitting mechanism occurs naturally in all of us, but most of us work through this if left on our own. We slowly realise that sometimes opposites coexist quite naturally. Think, for instance, of comedy. This often relies on reconciling opposites. For example, the Iranian comedian Omid Djalili jokes, "I am the only Iranian comedian in the world... and that's three more than Germany!" Whereas most people get this instinctively as funny, I have met many people who just don't get it. Likewise, the Woody Allen joke I referred to earlier, about the brother who thinks he's a chicken, causes many to become exasperated because they cannot grasp the humour.

Humour is an antidote to splitting because it allows for opposites to co-exist. Funnily enough, the WOKE religion is averse to humour. Perhaps it is no coincidence since Puritans are not renowned for joy and laughter. I often think back to the 'Blackadder II' episode called 'Beer', where Edmund Blackadder's puritanical relatives visit, coinciding with a drunken beer fest he has organised to please the Queen. The humour is there for all to see as we anticipate with relish, the inevitable meeting of these two sides of the 'split'. In Psychological Games, the switch reveals the split reality. Here are some examples of mind manipulations or 'Jedi Mind Tricks'. They are used to put us in a 'split' state.

- 'Good cop/Bad cop'

Often used by police to interrogate those with an antisocial personality; it aims to confuse the person by presenting them with a constantly changing narrative. Used in cults to exploit a split, as seduction follows coercion, then back again until the individual submits.

- **'Let's you and him fight'**

This is a well-known game in TA. It involves 'setting up' a fight between two parties, by mischievously telling each person bad things, purportedly said by the other behind their back. Then stepping back and watching the show... a 'playground fight'. Works particularly well with those of paranoid persuasion.

- 'If you're not with me (us)... you're against me (us).'

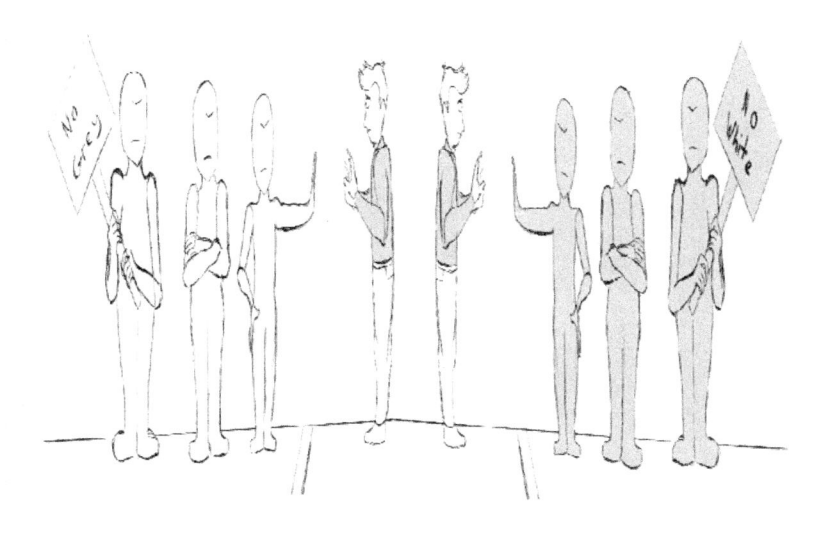

This is a divisive binary choice that attempts to coerce the other person - to 'shut up and obey!' 'Believe what we believe or you can't be friends with us.' Works particularly well with those brought up to be obedient towards power and authority.

- **'Let your hair down and live a little'**

"Here try these " or "Don't be such a prude" or "All your friends have done it."

This is a seductive, permission-giving message, designed to make the person appear 'cool' by breaking with their upbringing and adopting a new, promiscuous attitude. Often used to create a dominant sexual narrative. It is used to get the other to do something 'deviant', that they cannot go back from, as a prelude to joining the cult.

- 'Psychology 101'

One person uses their superior knowledge of psychology to manipulate another by telling them that they don't know anything - that they're 'projecting' or are 'in denial'. Misusing their deeper understanding of the psychological world, they delve into the 'unconscious world' of the other, redefining their truth and making them into a compliant puppet. Works well on those who have no independent, free thought.

- 'Righteous indignation' or 'Outrage'

This is often used on social media by SJWs who view themselves as 'morally superior'. They wish to impose their puritanical values on others, to make them feel inadequate and inferior. "That's outrageous" is a manipulation-by-definition; a more honest exchange would be as a statement of personal opinion, "I find it outrageous." Works well on the anxious or guilt-ridden individual.

- 'How could any sane person...?'

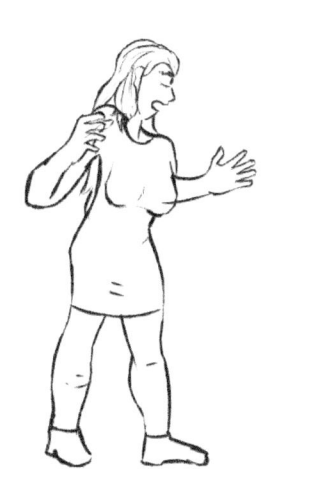

Manipulates by questioning how a person could believe such a preposterous thing. Often said in an "I can't believe it" way, with disbelief and emotion, often shouting. In other words, making a statement that defines sanity as you believing the same as them. Works well on those who have a felt need to please others.

- 'Teams'

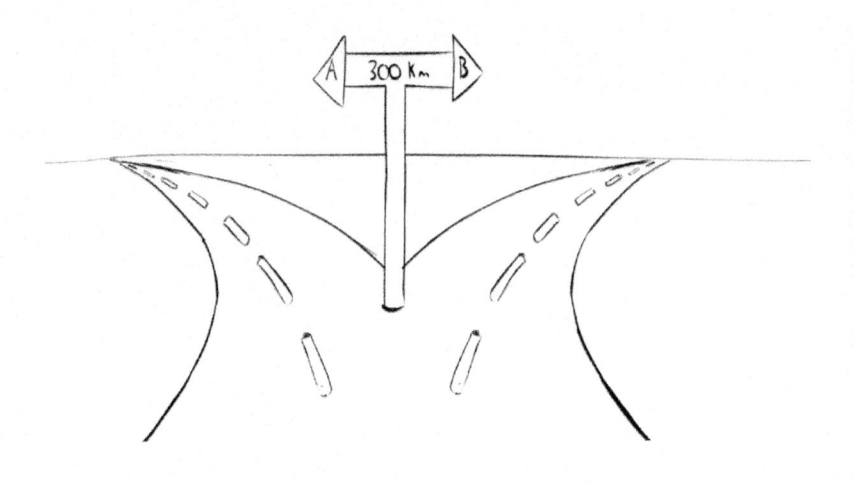

You EITHER belong to team A or Team B and there is no other choice. It's another example of a binary choice (which is no choice at all!) A politician's favourite all or nothing manipulation. Works well on the passive, those who want an easy, conflict-free life.

- 'Gas Lighting'

This is used to manipulate the situation to make the other person feel they cannot trust their reality and are going mad. This is a technique often employed by the married spouse, who has been caught cheating. Through denial and deceit, they succeed in getting the other to question their own sanity. Based on the film of that name, it involves a man trying to persuade his wife that she is going mad, by manipulating the gas lights. In cults, it is used to reinforce the belief that members can ONLY trust the cult!

- 'Odd girl out'

A straight-A student's life is slowly made a misery by her schoolmates, who tease and torment her in every way, both psychologically and physically. Slowly, she becomes more withdrawn, turning to self-harming and drugs. This plays on low self-confidence individuals who confuse their self-esteem with esteem-from-others. It's a form of shunning.

- **Trolling or One-person, multiple accounts**

This is found on social media platforms and relies on anonymity. One person has multiple accounts and can therefore artificially vote others up or down, inflating their vote. It gives a false impression of popularity, akin to voter fraud. Candace Owens, the black activist, developed an app that would expose who these trolls really were. She recalls an event where she was warned off, by a Twitter employee, from taking a position on 'lifting the mask off trolls'. Within 2 hours of her posting her piece, Candace had approx. 4,000 down votes all claiming to come from the political right, whereas they had come from left-wing trolls. The fraud is to do with faking popularity or unpopularity so that ordinary people are deceived. It is a variant of the modern game 'opinion polls'.

- **'Human shields'**

Originally this referred to the practice of placing women and children in harm's way as a 'shield' for the terrorists that hid behind them. The same technique is now used by political groups that use genuine plights of people to hide behind while pursuing their own agenda. The banner may read 'Righteous cause', but the secret agenda may be one of promoting violence, hatred and division. BLM and Antifa are examples.

- 'Intersectionality' – the enemy of my enemy is my friend.

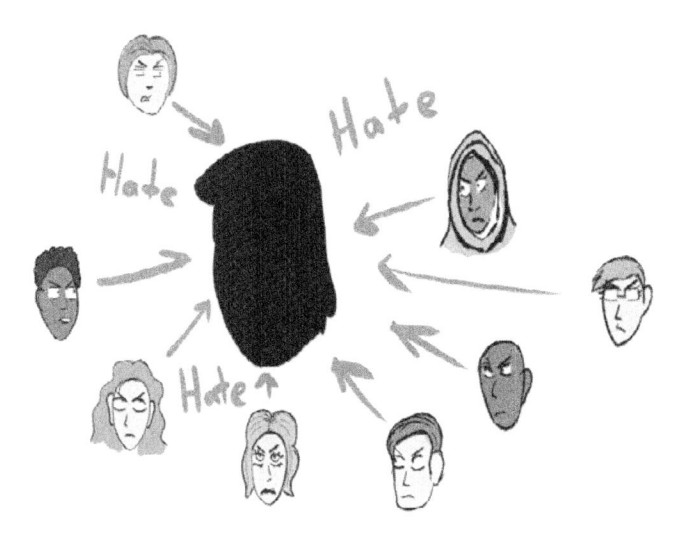

This involves forming a coalition against, rather than an alliance for, a particular project. It is not necessarily a group of people who are naturally drawn to one another. This can create in-fighting amongst members whose fundamental values may contradict those of other members. This is evident amongst Traditional Feminists and Trans, where some support biological women and view the stance of former biological males now identifying as trans, as putting men's rights before women's rights.

- **'I play, you pay'**

Think of a group of friends sharing the restaurant bill and some wanting to share the bill equally, whilst others want to divide it according to what each had. "I'm not paying the same as you, cos I only had a small X and you had a large Y." Worse still, if some walk off and leave the others to pay their bill... after all 'Responsibility' is an optional state of mind! This goes back to our different attitudes to what is considered 'Fair'.

- 'Too Big To Fail'

In 2008, bankers played casino gambling with the public's money, and they were bailed out from the public purse– this is different to the game of 'debtor', where one person would run up a debt and had to face the consequences. Nowadays, so many individuals run up a debt they cannot pay, that they collectively have to be bailed out, as they collectively have become too big to fail. Like 'Responsibility', 'Consequences' is an optional state of mind!

- **'No True Scotsman'**

Someone states "No true Scotsman would put sugar in his porridge." Someone else pipes up, "My uncle Hamish is from Aberdeen and he uses sugar in his." "Ach..." comes the reply, "but no TRUE Scotsman would use sugar instead of salt." This is all about 'he who defines, holds the power', a technique used to silence dissent. In the United Kingdom, a group of left-wing MPs recently wrote to the Home Secretary (who is of Ugandan-Indian heritage), complaining. According to the Guardian Newspaper,[77] "In the strongly worded letter, the MPs told the home secretary they were disappointed 'at the way you used your heritage and experiences of racism to gaslight the very real racism faced by black people and communities across the UK'". i.e. No TRUE minority voice would say that!

---

[77] (Guardian, 2020)

- **'Alternative Facts '**

Used by the media to 'put a spin' on their news narrative. By highlighting some items and downplaying others, the media can promote a message that suits its political agenda. This has led to calls of 'Fake news' in recent times.

- **Let's not go there!**

This is a technique used by news anchors to prevent guests from straying into territory that does not suit the news channel. It involves imposing censorship, while on live air, which will be a warning, followed by a break in transmission if it is not heeded.

- **So, what you're saying is...**

Expertly demonstrated by Cathy Newman during her interview with Jordan Peterson. Here, the interviewer inaccurately and deceitfully summarises what the guest has not said, and attempts to object to her own re-formulation of what she professes the guest said. Peterson famously deconstructed Cathy Newman's argument for all the world to see.

These are just some of the Jedi Mind Tricks used by those who wish to manipulate us into thinking along certain lines. **Here they are applied consciously and are manipulations.**

Reality TV is anything but that. It appears spontaneous, yet is heavily scripted and often is compulsive viewing. It uses psychological techniques such as those listed previously. Reality TV shows act as a way of creating often intense drama, compelling conflicts and inducing a manic state in the observer, who often gets immersed in what is unreal and manipulated TV.

These mind tricks, **when played unconsciously**, were originally called 'psychological games' by Dr Eric Berne in 'Games People Play'. Described here, they are manipulations. They clearly work better on some, but not all people. Why is that and where does Human Nature fit in?

Human Nature

Does man have an inherent nature or is he malleable? In TA, the concept of 'Life Script' goes a long way towards answering that question, in that it sees the child in his early years of development as susceptible to parental and other influences. The script is seen as 'decisional', something that can be changed through therapy, should the individual choose to apply themselves through personal agency. But then, there is the biological component, where individual temperament mitigates or aggravates that influence. Thus, in the Nature v Nurture debate[78], TA acknowledges both are important, yet sets out to help address the effects of lapses in nurture. Nature, however, is left largely unaddressed.

What is the nature of 'human nature'? Is there such a thing? Is man merely a 'Tabula rasa' or a blank slate? If so, can political activism act in place of personal agency to foster change? Are we hard-wired by our biology on issues of gender and race, or are we free to decide for instance our sexual orientation? Some believe it is sexual orientation that is hard-wired and that gender and race are decisional.

Is there an essential 'nature' template upon which nurture works her magic? If so, is this essence a vital component of human nature or are we just organisms that 'exist' with no intrinsic nature? There is considerable disagreement as to

---

[78] (Matt Ridley, 2003)

whether man is a sentient organism with a free will, or whether man is a mechanistic being, who can be externally reprogrammed. Is there any divinity therefore in man or are we no more than a product of biological evolution?

Roger Scruton, in his book 'Human Nature'[79], begins by distinguishing between the person and the Human Being. He believes that what characterises the person includes all that makes up the Human Being, but that there is a lot more besides. Personhood is a long way off from the animal kingdom since it is uniquely preserved for people. In that way, he allows for the Essence of being a person to stand apart from us being simply a more intelligent, Darwinian ape.

What about good and evil? Is man born good or evil? Are some people fundamentally good, and others evil? This question has been debated endlessly by philosophers, theologians, poets and psychologists. There is no consensus, some seeing in man an essential badness and requiring some level of constraint, others viewing man as naturally good and wanting him to be left alone. This fundamental question lies at the heart of the differences splitting our society apart.

Perhaps it is better to ask how inherent is essentialism in defining man's nature and to what extent is man's nature

---

[79] (Roger Scruton 2017)

for him to make of as he wishes? The divide in opinion goes back to the pessimistic view of Thomas Hobbes[80] who believed that in man's natural state, moral ideas do not exist. Thus, in speaking of human nature, he defines good simply as that which people desire and evil as that which they avoid, at least in the state of nature.

Jean-Jacques Rousseau[81] believed that man, by nature, is good and that people in the state of nature were innocent and at their best and that they were corrupted by the unnaturalness of civilization. This optimistic view inspires those who believe, that if 'the chains' imposed by civilisation are removed, people will assume their natural 'noble' state.

In Existentialism, Existence is always particular and individual. Humans are therefore called, in Martin Heidegger's phrase, Dasein[82] ("there being") because they are defined by the fact that they exist, or are in the world and inhabit it. Jean-Paul Sartre[83] popularised the view that 'Existence precedes essence', meaning that he believed that there was no inherent or essential human nature only existence. In other words, a 'blank slate'.

---

[80] (Thomas Hobbes, 1651)
[81] (Jean-Jacques Rousseau, 1755)
[82] (Martin Heidegger, 1927)
[83] (Jean-Paul Sartre, 1945)

The difference in opinion as to the nature of Human nature continues to divide us. David Berlinski[84] considers some aspects of being human as 'essential'. In his book on 'Human Nature', he clearly disagrees with Steven Pinker on the subject of violence. Pinker, in 'Enlightenment Now'[85], is at pains to promote his belief that violence in the twentieth century was not as bad as we might think, referring to homicide rates as evidence. Berlinski, an eminent mathematician, takes this apart, showing how ridiculous and frivolous Pinker's assertions are; that violence is an essential part of human nature and that violence cannot be wished or washed away. Wishful thinking will not eliminate violence.

And, it is on the subject of whether man is inherently a violent creature or a peaceful one that so much disagreement resides. The subject of whether violence can be a force for good underpins psycho-political bodies such as BLM and Antifa[86]. They believe so passionately that their cause is a just and good one, that they are prepared to countenance the use of force in pursuit of their agendas. Interestingly, the KKK and the Brownshirts and Blackshirts used the same arguments to pursue their agendas. By contrast, Gandhi and Martin Luther King Jr used peaceful

---

[84] (David Berlinski, 2019)
[85] (Steven Pinker, 2018)
[86] (Mark Bray, 2017)

protest to achieve their political aims, preferring persuasion to coercion.

The argument as to whether existence or essence is more important is perhaps too binary. Surely, each contributes to who we are. We each have the potential to do good, but also a capacity to do harm... especially if we forget that we are people and instead pursue an ideologically-driven agenda.

In his book, 'The Still Small Voice', Donald Carveth[87] reminds us of the need for a conscience that is based on more than reason. He believes that in human history, more damage has been done by ideology-driven than by pathologically-driven brutality. Even if each individual person manages to overcome their violent tendencies, what happens when they are required to act as a group? What if they are called upon to defend the vulnerable from an external threat, from a brutal, violent force that wishes to annihilate them? Has their capacity for violence been removed or simply de-activated and put to sleep?

Winston Churchill[88] pondered on such questions. He was aware that the British military would be required to repulse an enemy that was intent on annihilating them. He did not question whether people would be willing to die for their

---

[87] (Donald Carveth, 2013)
[88] (Larry Arnn, 2015)

country, for many had been willing to sacrifice their own lives in the service of war. He did however formulate this differently; as to whether they would be willing to kill to save Britain! This is altogether a different prospect and one that many fail to take into account. Dead bodies do not push back against those with murderous intent – are we seriously imagining a world where EVERYONE is incapable of violence or is this a futile hope?

Are we fundamentally naïve and innocent or are we aware of our own shortcomings and the dangers posed by those that mean us harm? Has postmodernism switched us off to real dangers and distracted us onto imaginary dangers instead?

A Conflict of visions

In 'A conflict of visions', Thomas Sowell[89] discusses a topic that gets to the heart of political, social, psychological and other world view splits that are evident in the modern Western world. He defines a vision as a 'pre-analytic cognitive act' – a felt sense of something before applying reason or logic. A Vision is not the same as a wish or a dream. Instead, it incorporates the assumptions we often unconsciously hold when we think. Visions underpin our understanding of the world and Sowell compares the 'constrained' vision of the American Revolution, with the 'unconstrained' vision of the French revolution. The difference centres on how one views human nature. The constrained vision sees man as essentially flawed, a mixture of good and bad. Therefore, society needs institutions that keep individuals from committing harm and institutions that are kept in check by a separation of powers. These checks and balances are essential if society values freedom. Hence, the conservatives favour ideas such as setting limits, freedom of speech, boundaries, law and order and constitution.

In the 'unconstrained vision, man is seen as an essentially malleable creature, with harm and pathology being largely social constructs. Institutions should exist to liberate the

---

[89] (Thomas Sowell, 2007)

human spirit and help him aspire to his unflawed state. Socialists or collective liberals see no need for institutions that curb one's freedoms, only enhance them and promote equality. There is no need for separation of powers or checks and balances, only leaders that are 'philosopher kings' or elites.

The French Revolution ended with the guillotine and Napoleon Bonaparte. Yet it keeps being reborn in socialist politics and the exuberance of youth. The American Revolution gave rise to the American constitution, the conservation of independence and freedom, and the success of capitalism.

In 'A conflict of visions' Sowell shows just how different the world views are, and how they lead to incompatible policies. As idealism clashes with realism, we have the conflict between Plato's vision and that of Aristotle.

Another way to view this is to contrast the ideologies that were behind the last two world wars. Namely, the German Ideology versus that of 'The West'. The Ideology of the West can best be summed up as the ideas of 1789—liberalism, individualism, constitutionalism, and droits de l'homme (Human Rights). The German Ideology, in contrast, was based on 'Sonderweg' or special path. This has a visceral hostility to the ideas of Western 'Universalism' or there being one fundamental Truth. Influenced by thinkers such as Hegel, Nietzsche, Feuerbach, Marx and Engels, the German ideology took root in the twentieth century and was in opposition to the 1789 enlightenment position. It valued organisation, collectiveness and power, emphasising values such as 'fate', 'decisiveness', 'struggle' and 'destiny', over those of liberal 'Christianity' [90]. Thus, the two opposing visions led both to WW1 and WW2. In 2020, we are once again seeing these two very different world views in opposition, with the Woke movement basing itself on the culturally popular German vision, which is anti-capitalistic and promotes a welfare state. They stand for Freedom of the Collective. In contrast, the Awake group holds on to the historically successful 1789 values, which advocate for free markets and capitalism. They stand for Freedom of the Individual.

---

[90] (Colin Wolin, 2016)

The naïve optimism of liberal ideology

After the Second World War, there was a 'cold war' between the USA and the USSR. Many called this a Bipolar world, a fight between a Liberal democracy and a Socialist autocracy. With the fall of the Berlin Wall in 1989, many hailed it as a victory for Liberal values, democracy and Freedom. It was even touted as 'the end of history'. Yet optimism forgot the brutality shown by the Chinese Communist Party in Tiananmen Square in June 1989.

In the Nineties, there was optimism that Liberalism, Democracy and Capitalism were uncontested victors. The USA under Bill Clinton promoted the inclusion of Communist China into the World Trade Organisation. The thinking was an optimistic one, for it was thought that by accepting Capitalism, China would in time become less autocratic and more democratic. The goal was to create a Liberal China. This wish now appears naïve and more like wishful thinking. Instead of being converted by the liberal and democratic world views, China has imposed its anti-democratic (e.g. Hong Kong) and autocratic dogma (e.g. by coercing nations such as Australia to its will) on the Western world. The communist party in China, like its predecessor the USSR, has utilised postmodern thought to manipulate Western modernist thought. China is often worshipped by the global establishment as the replacement to the USA, by those who are dissatisfied with democracy and traditional liberalism.

Postmodern philosophies are irrational left-wing ideologies, packaged to sound less unreasonable[91]. They are based less on reason and thought and more on feeling and assertion. During the French Revolution, those in charge grappled with many such ways of thinking. They fought to impose a new vision of Freedom, called Positive Freedom.[92] This is the freedom to live without constraints rather than the Freedom from the tyranny of government. What later emerged was that freedom from constraints was an idealistic slogan; for who constrains the crowd when it acts against the vulnerable citizen?

Positive Freedom appealed to the crowd, who were told that they were being kept 'in shackles' by the state; that the state had to be replaced not reformed. The crowd manipulators streamed in Rousseau's now-famous line, **'man is born free, but he is everywhere in chains'**,[93] which challenged the traditional order of society. As their grievances were highlighted and exploited, those in the crowd were told that all they had to do was break these 'chains' and rebel to gain their 'natural' freedom. Hence, the crowd set France on fire! Those manipulating the crowd

---

[91] (Stephen Hicks, 2013)
[92] (Isaiah Berlin, 1958)
[93] (Jean-Jacques Rousseau, 1762)

knew that their child-like, magical seductions, appealed to those who held grievances. Instead of reason, the crowd manipulators used poetic licence to rile the crowd - Those leading the mob promoted the idea that the King and those in power held the poor in contempt. The now-famous saying, "Let them eat cake," attributed to the French Queen Marie Antoinette, has gone down in the annals of history. Its poetic simplicity acted as a slogan with which to inflame the passions of the revolutionaries. Eventually, it led to the 'Terror' and the 'Guillotine'. As the crowd burned down the old structures, they eliminated the monarchy, reduced the influence of the clergy and established the First Republic. However, as with all postmodern ideologies, it was easier to tear down the establishment, than to establish a better one. France is now in its Fifth Republic, incarnation after incarnation failing to find a version that truly lives up to its expectations: 'Liberté, égalité, fraternité'. This slogan is again based on poetic licence and does not hold together as common sense. Liberty and equality can be contradictory. Likewise, brotherhood (fraternité) is about the collective, whilst traditional formulations of liberty had their roots in individualism. Little wonder then that France struggles, to this day, to give true expression to its national slogan.

The strength of Postmodernist philosophies lies in their seductive-yet-superficial analyses or picking apart whatever they address, be it rival philosophies, world views or governing principles - in short, any modernist philosophies.

However, they do this by appealing to infantile, destructive impulses, unconstrained by any long-term considerations. By ignoring reason and logic in A$_2$, as well as knowledge, history and wisdom in P$_2$, they press the accelerator pedal and forget the brakes! Where they fail is in achieving any real sense of consensus as to their alternative final outcome. Just as in the French Revolution, it was all about destruction without being able to agree on what the final vision would look like. Instead of reforming society, postmodern philosophies go for broke.

Constructionism, Deconstructionism and Nihilism are three postmodern doctrines that each have a seductive-yet-oversimplistic way of viewing the world. Each provides a prism of thought and each provides child-like, magical thinking that attacks the central pillars of Modernism, namely Truth, Reason and Knowledge.

Postmodernism appeals more to public sentiment and less to personal feeling - The collective rather than the individual. In getting caught up in the mood of the crowd, anyone can forget to take their own personal fear and reservations into account. Hence the 'terror', where the masses embarked on an orgy of torture and killings that eventually consumed the original ringleaders. There was no personal conscience that got in the way. What the group had was a collective will of its own – a 'madness of crowds'. Believing that what they were doing was 'right' they did great evil and irreparable harm. **In the name of their ideology, they set aside their common humanity and exterminated those who were different.**

So, the thing to say about postmodernism is that it will seem mad to the modernist. It is not based on common sense only mass hysteria. The postmodernist will apply a different set of rules to thought itself – where all truths are subjective - and seek to destroy the ancient gods of modernism. As the traditional institutions fall, they will cheer and claim victory. Only, it is a short-lived victory at best. The question is what will replace what was?

China is now beginning to cause us to ask questions. Was liberalism naïve to believe in its own success? Are we being turned more into China, than China is being Westernised? The world is on the brink as we begin to reassess our decision in the nineties. Have we allowed ourselves to sleepwalk into an authoritarian, or possibly totalitarian nightmare?

The End of History

Francis Fukuyama's book 'The End of History and the Last Man'[94] gives us a blueprint for what has happened to the West since the 1990s.

He argues that with the victory of Western Liberal Democracy, following the Cold War (1945–1991) and the breakup of the Soviet Union (USSR) humanity has reached "not just... the passing of a particular period of post-war history, but the end of history as such: That is, the end-point of mankind's ideological evolution and the universalization of Western liberal democracy as the final form of human government." In the book, he expands on his essay, "The End of History?" (1989). Fukuyama draws upon the ideologies and philosophies of Hegel and Marx. In his opinion, they define human history as a linear progression, from one socio-economic epoch to another.

Far from viewing the USA as the victor, he put forward yet another socialist vision for the West, based on the European Union. He later expanded on his views: "The End of History was never linked to a specifically American model of social or political organization. Following Alexandre Kojeve, the Russian-French philosopher who inspired my original argument, I believe that the European Union more accurately reflects what the world will look like at the end

---

[94] (Francis Fukuyama, 1992)

of history than the contemporary United States. The EU's attempt to transcend sovereignty and traditional power politics by establishing a transnational rule of law is much more in line with a "post-historical" world than the Americans' continuing belief in God, national sovereignty and their military."

This view has dominated the Western governments since the nineties. Yet more recently, the European Union has been shown to be little more than a utopian dream, with Britain voting to leave it in 2016. However, many people continue to wish to remain in this dream, despite it being riddled with so many obvious flaws. The wish that the EU would be the model for a better future for all mankind, lies in shambles, yet another failed socialist project.

As Western governments attempt to impose the Fukuyama vision on their people, they deny and defy the very nature of being human. That whereas some people are willing to surrender their personal freedoms to some authoritarian, supranational world order, many people will refuse and fight for their individual freedom, democracy and anti-slavery attitudes.

Like so many postmodernists, Fukuyama fails to acknowledge that persuasion alone will not lead us all to his utopian destination. Instead, it is a totalitarian future that he advocates. The new destination for the West is undoubtedly Communist China and a resurgent America must be defeated for the illiberal project to succeed. Will they succeed by denying people their voice and their vote? The New World Order has a fight on its hands.

The Plutocracy

Up until recently, anyone who believed that the world was being run by unaccountable elites and big business, would have been called a 'conspiracy theorist'. However, so bold has the World Economic Forum become, that it has published its agenda for the future of mankind, under the name 'The Big Reset'[95]. This is yet another socialist project, that promises to bring the world together in a Fourth Industrial Revolution. It is full of very bold edicts. What is different is that the establishment has changed sides. The left is now in hock to big business.

Under the guise of a 'Green' agenda,[96] it imposes a corporate vision on us all. It is a future where private property will disappear, yet where we will all be 'happier'; where we all welcome refugees yet corporations will still be able to make profits. A centralised world where individual liberty will be sacrificed on the altar of collective freedom. There will no longer be nations, but a world government. The establishment has become postmodernist.

Upset by the rise in the Populist, Nationalist pushback against their Fukuyama plan, those that view themselves as our betters have given up on us. Democracy is viewed as a

---
[95] (Klaus Schwab & Thierry Malleret, 2020)
[96] (Rupert Darwall, 2019)

failed system because too many of us voted against their pet projects; namely the European Union and the inevitable decline of the USA. China has escaped criticism for unleashing the Covid-19 virus. Instead, it was the cause of the National lockdown throughout the world, the cause of the collapse of successful economies, and the signal that the plutocracy meant to end this populist revolt. When all this is over, Trump will no longer be in office and Boris will be moved aside in preparation for an even more compliant 'Prime Minister'. What we will be left with is a new world, that the plutocracy prefers. A world where we lose our individuality, our human rights and everything that made us a free people under capitalism. There will no longer be nations, but a New World Order to which we must submit.

The Corporate world will use more propaganda to convince the many gullible people by appealing to their sentiments. Some dictators would be proud to see how the plutocracy has pulled this off. But, it didn't turn out that well for AH in the end. P_1 did not overpower P_2.

Yet, in all this scheming and corporate greed, they forget that human nature will always contain contradictions. That an imposed vision is not the same as one arrived at organically. That totalitarianism is not something that everyone is happy to live under. They have ignored or forgotten the writings of George Orwell and Aldous Huxley.

Instead, they have used '1984' and 'Brave New World' as a blueprint for their utopian vision. How deluded they are.

The world turned upside down.

People are full of internal contradictions. Yet, learning how to integrate and hold together these contradictory aspects of ourselves is a vital part of the psychotherapeutic journey. Living with tension is a sign that we're alive. We don't resolve a split by ignoring its opposite or by pretending that it doesn't exist. Indoctrination will not convince everyone. Then what?

In TA psychotherapy, an A_2 is vital. Before any meaningful work can begin, the therapist and client need to establish a baseline as to what constitutes Reality. Otherwise, without this vital first step, there can be no therapeutic contract nor any agreement on a treatment plan. The effort to create an A_2 space first, before entering the fantasy world of the Child, is called DECONTAMINATION. New TA practitioners sometimes forget that fact, and enthusiastically enter the world of the Child too soon. Before long, however, they realise that they have become as lost as their client. Because they have not differentiated between the world of objectivity, reason and fact, and that of passion, subjectivity and assertion, there is no agreed, consensual reality to check things out with. How do, for instance, paranoid thoughts get differentiated from more healthy ones? How do obsessive-compulsive issues become identified and addressed if the person continues to justify them? How is violence believed to be justifiable... or that some people are better than others? Decontamination is the process whereby Child and/or Parent ego states are not allowed to contaminate the A₂ space. P₂ and C₂ are pushed out of the A₂ space into their separate areas. They are not eliminated, simply kept out.

Decontamination does not address the content in each ego state. That comes later, in a process called Deconfusion. What decontamination does is to separate out the content into three distinct areas, like putting matching furniture in different rooms in a house. That way, the impulses that belong to the Child are recognised as such and kept separate from the more mature Adult processes. Likewise, exogenous Parental material is also kept out of Adult.

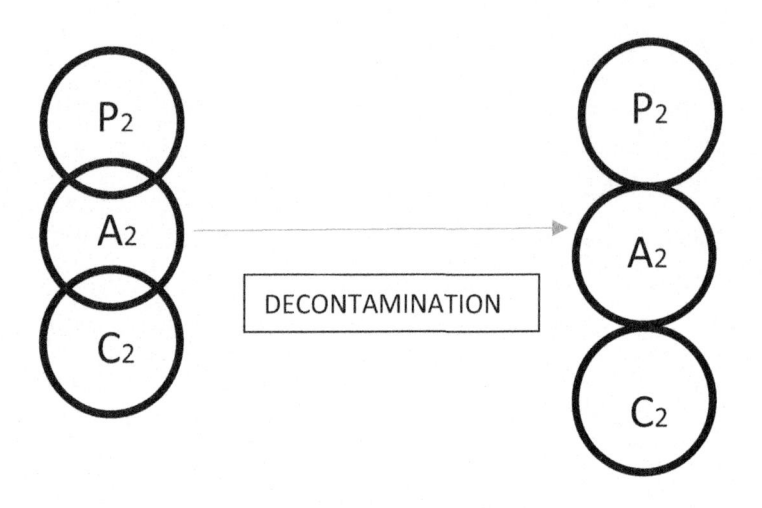

DECONTAMINATION

A_2 is a space where the client can reflect on their thoughts and feelings, contemplate their actions, analyse their transactions and games, go to when things get confusing or overwhelming, separate feelings from sentiments and begin to appreciate 'the other' in relationships. Without a decontaminated Adult ego state, no meaningful psychotherapy can take place. If instead of A_2, all that happens is taking place in C_2, there is no learning and no corrective actions taken to address the personality structure. The client may 'feel better' because their biases are being reinforced instead of challenged, yet at what cost? Allowing the client to continue believing that their problems are the fault of others is antitherapeutic since it does not confront the illusions, delusions and confusions that the client presents with. Also, by only dealing with the primitive world of P_1, A_1 and C_1, the client is being kept infantile, never to develop a real Adult A_2 ego state.

Additionally, since the postmodernist movement streams in a P_1 Parent ego state, followers never see the need to check things out with those that present challenging and alternative opinions. By insisting on a PC viewpoint of the world, revisionist history and a carefully-sanitised version of 'the truth', their database is dangerously biased and unrealistic. They do not develop an independent P_2 Parent ego state with which to balance their Child impulses.

Transactional Analysis was born during the Civil Rights movement in the USA in the 1960s. It reached the heights of its ambition in the 1980s when there were thousands of TA practitioners and it aimed to encourage a well-rounded, balanced personality. Since then, the arrival of postmodernism has resulted in an overblown Child ego state and a reduction or elimination of A_2 and P_2. This is popularly referred to as the 'narcissistic style' or the 'it's all about ME generation'. Narcissism is characterised by a False persona covering a Real self. Thus, the virtuous self that is on display, is often at odds with the real self, lurking underneath. For instance, someone posting warm, fuzzy messages on social media, may really be a cruel and cold-hearted individual in disguise.

Ego states can be drawn to show how the PAC structure has changed since Eric Berne first conceptualised Transactional Analysis in the 1950s. The world then was very different, with an overblown Parent and very little Child. By the mid-eighties, the well-rounded personality was considered a more balanced individual, and the destination aimed for in psychotherapy. By 2020 however, we are seeing an overblown Child with virtually no Parent and a reduced Adult. Many Universities now resemble traditional churches, with dogma replacing a variety of opinions, challenging ideas being cancelled and where the worship of 'humanity' has replaced that of God. Postmodern Indoctrination has replaced education in many cases.

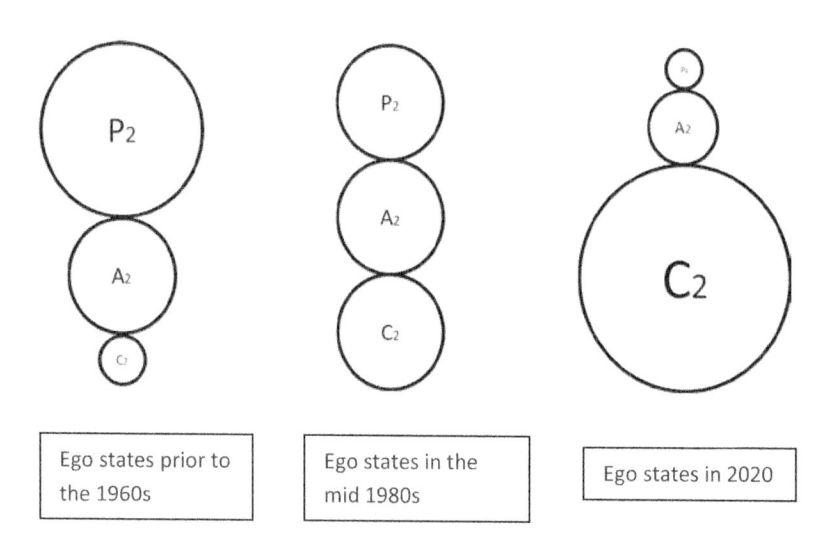

| Ego states prior to the 1960s | Ego states in the mid 1980s | Ego states in 2020 |

The last diagram illustrates the divide we are experiencing in the Western world. Those who identify as WOKE can best be represented by the 2020 ego state diagram. Those who identify as AWAKE probably relate better to both the ego states before the 1960s AND to the ego states in the mid-1980s. It would not be an accurate representation to think of traditionalists as all being 'old folk', since many relate to the balanced ego state model as one that still makes the best sense. Those who identify as 'classic liberal' would relate to the centre diagram, and long for a return to a world that is balanced and makes sense. A world where the achievement of the Civil Rights movement can be honoured and celebrated. Instead, as Douglas Murray has said in his book, 'The Madness of Crowds'[97], "Women's rights had – like gay rights – been steadily accumulated throughout the twentieth century. They too appeared to be arriving at some sort of settlement. Then just as the train appeared to be reaching its desired destination it suddenly picked up steam and went crashing off down the tracks and into the distance." In place of settling for **equality**, they have tasted power, and gone for **mastery** instead.

The intersectional world of WOKE includes many minority groups that have come together under a 'progressive' umbrella. Yet, many 'progressive' feminists are at odds with 'traditional' feminists. Many 'progressive' gay-rights representatives are at odds with 'traditional' gay-rights representatives. Likewise, 'progressive' black supporters are at odds with 'traditional' black supporters. The only group that does not have a 'traditional' voice, is the recently formed 'Trans' movement. This is the group that has acquired a voice and a status as a result of it being promoted by the intersectional movement. It is being weaponised and being used to lead in their vanguard assault on Individualism and Traditionalism. The other side has nothing to repel them with and is being called 'transphobic'. This in itself is another contradiction, since the word 'phobic' invokes

---

[97] (Douglas Murray, 2019)

pathology and Woke intersectionalists are meant to sympathise with their 'mental health' brethren; they should not dismiss or denigrate them, and certainly not see them as 'bad'.

The postmodernist philosophies thus look at the world in ways that turn the world inside out and upside down.

Empathy

I would like to return to the topic of 'empathy' since I believe that it may be at the heart of so much current misconception and misunderstanding. It is often sold as a good quality to have, both by psychotherapists and politicians. Angela Merkel referred to a 'lack of empathy' in justifying her decision to allow over a million migrants into Germany in 2015. Yet the criticism she subsequently received, despite praise in some quarters, indicated that her actions had breached the Golden Rule when it came to her own citizens and other EU countries.

"But coming to **know** how the other feels (empathic identification) is not at all the same thing as the sympathy (sympathetic identification) that moves beyond knowing to **caring**."[98] Sympathy is about more than simply knowing. It is about **caring** or giving a damn.

Empathy is then not the moral good that many of us think it is. "The sadist must empathise with his victims in order to enjoy their suffering. So **for moral action to occur empathy is not enough**. It is one thing to know that others suffer; quite another to care and desire to relieve their pain."[99]

---

[98] (Donald Carveth, 2018) – my emphasis in bold
[99] (Donald Carveth, 2018) – my emphasis in bold

The most common mistake is to think of empathy as a deep concept and to dismiss sympathy as a shallow one. It is the other way round. Using Empathy, we may end up knowing too much yet caring too little. It comes about as a result of misunderstanding Kohut's Self-Psychology.[100]

Robert Berezin[101] considers that "Empathy has been revered as the emotional analogue of wisdom." He considers that it is "vastly overrated." Empathy is different from compassion. The former is a form of 'projective identification' and is full of inherent bias. It is 'a gun that points both ways', according to Paul Bloom[102]. For, in identifying with one group, who we might be attracted to (the poor, suffering, disadvantaged, people from a foreign culture), we may be biased against another, (a poor, suffering, disadvantaged group from our own culture). The white sub-group from the Appalachias, that voted for Trump in their droves[103], was white and poor, yet had been overlooked by Democratic politicians. Why were they ignored? It appears as if some politicians did not 'empathise' with the plight of ALL poor people. This is the problem with empathy. It appeals to our sense of moral goodness, but it is a biased sense, reserved only for people we are drawn to.

---

[100] (Heinz Kohut, 1971)
[101] (Robert Berezin, 2015)
[102] (Paul Bloom, 2017)
[103] (James David Vance, 2016)

A 'teacher's pet' situation, where one pupil is preferred over another, for no reason other than prejudice.

"In reality, empathy is actually - projective self-involvement," says Robert Berezin in 'Empathy is a False God'[104]. "This is ultimately a form of narcissism that passes as caring. The real caring item is best described as 'Responsiveness'. Responsiveness is a process of emotional receptivity, by which one is directly tuned into and involved with the other person with no reference to oneself at all. It does not involve identifying with the other person. It is a form of resonance with feeling itself. This capacity and its origins all come from maternal love. The mother responds directly to her baby's needs without any reference to herself. She is and always was, tuned into the baby's physical and emotional states directly. This is the source of all love. As a psychotherapist, the issue in therapy is responsiveness, not empathy." Thus, empathy is not the rare, wonderful quality we imagine it to be... and it is open to abuse and manipulation by sociopaths and psychopaths.

In the UK, Bob Geldof shamed the UK and the rest of the Western world into giving to his Charity Live Aid. Using Michael Buerk's 1984 BBC film, showing the poor in Ethiopia, he mobilised public sentiment. The poor in Africa were those, who we were told, we had to empathise with...

---

[104] (Robert Berezin, 2015)

and to forget the plight of the poor in our own country. Many UK charities received less money following this movement, but 'empathy' did not care so much about our own citizens who were suffering.

"In a divided world, empathy is not the solution, it is the problem; a source of prejudice, not kindness. We think of empathy – the ability to feel the suffering of others for ourselves – as the ultimate source of all good behaviour. But while it inspires care and protection in personal relationships, it has the opposite effect in the wider world."[105]

Paul Bloom views empathy as leading us to do both good and evil in its name. Defining empathy as feeling what another person is feeling, he sets about to demonstrate how it leads to biased decisions, can be dumb and even racist. Whilst empathy can lead to decisions that benefit our immediate family, friends and neighbours, it is poor when it comes to those outside of our sight zone. That in trying to do good, we can often do more harm than good. It is a poor predictor of moral goodness, political affiliation and worldview. Paul Bloom builds a case for rational compassion, where we use our heads as well as our hearts. He questions empathy's use in politics, in empathising with one group against another. He views empathy as something

---

[105] (Paul Bloom, 2017)

that can be manipulated by politicians to get us to feel the plight of certain groups while cutting off from feeling the plight of others.

We are experiencing a political weaponization of 'empathy' to justify the imposition of otherwise dubious political and social control measures. The central place afforded to empathy in politicised humanism has led to a worldwide movement of well-intentioned people who may have been sold a Goebbelsian 'big lie'.

There is, contrary to the much-touted hype, very little actual 'settled science' behind many of the left's assertions. The late Christopher Booker[106] found a lot of 'groupthink' pronouncements behind much of the public's acceptance of the 'Global Warming agenda'; now called 'Climate Change' because there has not been the predicted large increase in global temperatures, nor the extinction of the polar bear. Likewise, he challenged the political orthodoxy when it came to issues such as the European Union and the Paris Climate Agreement. He argued that Political Correctness and Groupthink dominated these agendas, and prevented proper challenge and debate. It has become customary to dismiss those promoting contrary ideas and opinions by labelling them 'deniers', a term that was originally used to denounce anyone who did not accept the church doctrine.

---

[106] (Christopher Booker, 2018, 2020)

Hiding behind the 'shield of empathy', it has become 'virtuous' to post 'sentiment-inducing' messages on social media, often now referred to as 'virtue signalling'. Something that has some potential good in it, namely empathy, is susceptible to psychological manipulation, through its prejudicial use. A spell may have been cast over the populace, who do not remain sceptical enough, in the face of herd mentality. We must wake up to that if nothing else.

Empathy and the Immersive Experience

Carveth turns his critique of empathy on psychotherapy itself. He says, "Our patients are often rightly suspicious of our empathic technique for they know that empathy and caring are two quite different things. To move significantly beyond empathy to genuine sympathy and reparative action requires…the integration and containment of one's childhood pain as opposed to splitting it off and inducing (projectively identifying) it into the other, the scapegoat."[107] As psychotherapists we must resist the urge to see ourselves in our clients, to projectively identify with them. Instead, we must care and wish to help them with their plight without getting lost in their world.

The danger with empathy is that as we get immersed in the imaginal world of our client, we lose touch with whose

---

[107] (Donald Carveth, 2018)

imagination it is we are dealing with; theirs or ours? In projective identification, it is our imagination that substitutes for the imagination of the client. We might care for the part of the client that reminds us of ourselves while remaining unknowing and uncaring about the parts of the client that we fail to recognise or sympathise with.

The immersive experience is a potentially dangerous one for the Empath. It takes over and can switch us off from the dangers that lurk therein. Believing that we empathise with the other and know their mind and intentions can be a delusional comfort. It is what Robert Berezin [108] wrote about when he was hoodwinked by a client who presented as the 'victim' of domestic abuse, yet who secretly wished to use him for her benefit. While, at first, he believed himself to be a good empathic therapist, he soon realised that he was being seduced into believing what she wanted him to believe. He was being seduced into not initially paying any attention to her secret agenda. That is, she was playing mind tricks and engaging him in mind manipulation for her own benefit. When he refused to play, her coercive side manifested and she accused him of " not caring about her hungry baby." Eventually, she owned up to her scam.

The immersive experience is also one used by video game designers, social media platforms and modern

---

[108] (Robert Berezin, 2015)

communication systems. They prey upon our brain's limbic system by artificially giving us shots of dopamine for pleasure.[109] Once caught up by the chemical addiction to 'getting likes', we find it very difficult to get off social media or to leave the virtual world and return to the 'real world'. Big Tech companies have exploited this human vulnerability and were aware of the addictive and relationship-destroying effect that people would be subjected to when they designed their products. Just as in the case of Tobacco companies and their products such as cigarettes, they just didn't give a damn.

Empathic immersion is a concept now being promoted in the field of 'Virtual Reality'.[110] Once again, it is being sold as a good thing; that somehow people with autism can develop empathy with others as a result of this new technology.[111] In my experience, people with ASD have too much empathy not too little. Instead, they easily get lost and confused in the world of others and cannot separate their own experiences from those of others. They struggle with individuation and relationships as a result. To get them caught up in ever more immersive experiences, risks them losing all touch with the 'real world' and becoming dependent on online experiences for all their interactions.

---

[109] (Simon Parkin, 2018)
[110] (Fernanda Herrera et al, 2018)
[111] (Jorge Herrero et al, 2019)

Similarly, empathic immersion is being seen as a positive way of getting the gamer to experience the world through the eyes of a minority group such as BAME. That is dangerously biased as if all BAME people think and feel the same. This is yet another extension of the 'unconscious bias training' projects, viewing all minorities as victims with which all right-minded people should feel 'empathy'. Once again, empathy and immersion are being sold as a product to get us to change our thinking. This is nothing more than postmodernist marketing of misinformed psychological concepts, much as they do with 'settled science'. They fail to sympathise or care about the ill effects these have on people as they peddle their ideology to unsuspecting, naïve and well-meaning people.

The immersive experience and virtual reality are training us to accept a virtual world instead of a real one. The same can be said of the Lockdown world we are forced to endure in 2020 because so many people have been scared witless and believe they face death if they venture outside. The virtual world is eerily similar to the world of 'The Matrix', where real people are trapped in womb-like cocoons and fed artificial intelligence programmes or simulated realities. They become slaves as their limbic system is stimulated with make-believe scenarios, similar to being immersed in a video game. All the while, their masters lurk in the corridors of power, unseen and untouchable.

Reaction Formation

There is a little understood or talked about defence mechanism in psychoanalysis. It is nowadays so widespread that it covers those afflicted, with a veil of 'moral goodness'. It is called Reaction Formation, a way of trying to deal with internal anxiety and guilt, by fixating on an idea or a feeling or desire, that is **the opposite of a feared unconscious impulse**. For instance, a mother who bears an unwanted child may react to her feeling of guilt for not wanting the child, by becoming extremely solicitous and overprotective to convince both the child and herself that she is a good mother. It is a form of psychological compensation.

What Shakespeare put so well in Hamlet, "The lady doth protest too much, methinks."[112]

Often, the person who develops a reaction formation will go overboard in trying to convince others that they are not this thing that they fear they are or know they are. Examples include:

A person who struggles to keep their anger under control goes out of their way to appear helpful and courteous to others, while not really feeling kind or courteous.

---
[112] (William Shakespeare, 1601)

A person who is deeply depressed goes out of their way to appear fun and happy, and not let others know how unhappy he really is.

A person who has authoritarian impulses, adopts a 'love and peace' persona, to disguise the contempt under which he really holds people.

Puritanism has 'reaction formation' at its core. Instead of feeling anxiety and guilt, reaction formation puts out a false 'goody-goody' narrative to disguise its true calling. By calling others out as 'bad', it staves off the internal feelings that it cannot grapple with. Psychologically, it is a mess, that only sees mess outside of itself, for those affected often experience an 'urge to purge', a type of compulsion. So, they fixate on a 'moral crusade', trying to rid the rest of us of something very dark in their own core. This amounts to trying to purge a sin in a saint, instead of healing the sin in their own heart. Think of the 'reformed smoker' to get an idea of what this mechanism is all about. Their puritanical zeal to stop everyone else from smoking, just because they have given up.

The modern left's version of humanism can be traced back to Germany, the place where psychoanalysis was born, as well as Nazi ideology. The Nazis were puritans who sought to purge the world of lesser humans, those they considered 'useless eaters' or 'life unworthy of life', *Lebensunwertes*

Leben[113]. The obedient populace was convinced by the brutality and the brainwashing of the Nazis to adopt a 'morally superior' stance. However, why did the German people fall for it? The answer may lie in 'Reaction Formation'. By fixating on an idea such as Nazi ideology, the people were provided with what A N Wilson[114] calls a 'consolation myth' - That their 'struggle' had not been in vain. For the Germans had endured severe hardship following the First World War, had seen atrocities and many deaths due to starvation. They had suffered much. However, in getting behind the purge of the Nazi movement, they were able to forget the past, and look ahead to a brighter future... where they could put their troubles behind them.

Only, instead of facing up to their own hell, they would bring that same hell to the rest of mankind; and in trying to escape their own guilt for the part played by Germany in the last world war, they may once again, be engaging in reaction formation!

Shelby Steele, the author of 'White Guilt'[115], speaks of collective guilt felt by the white community in America as it has wrestled with its history of racism. Even though it has acknowledged the sins of the past, guilt ensures that it can

---

[113] (Karl Binding & Alfred Hoche, 1920)
[114] (Andrew Norman Wilson, 2017)
[115] (Shelby Steele, 2007)

never forgive itself. There is no redemption narrative. The same could be said of Germany's 'war guilt', for instead of forgiving itself, it has adopted a reformed smoker stance. It must be on the constant lookout for any perceived signs of moral wickedness and act to stamp it out. This then is reaction formation once again. In trying to get rid of the disease, it imposes a cure that is still puritanical.

Those that felt anxious and guilty at their own authoritarian impulses projected those impulses into some of the innocent public, who they then sought to purge of it: **I see in thee, what is really in me, but I prefer not to look there. Instead, I shall see the badness as outside of me, for it has nothing to do with me, and everything to do with thee.** This is once again, the stance of the Paranoid Schizophrenic.

With its roots in Reaction Formation, the left has embarked on a crusade that it cannot win... however, it is prepared to burn everything down on a crazy misconception, a fixation that is dishonest at its core; the belief that other people are bad, and either must be purged of their sins or must perish, is as old as the hills. 'Repent or Perish'.

It was and still is, the cause of hatred of Jews or anti-Semitism. It is little wonder that so much hatred exists for Jews, especially those who were finally given a home following the Holocaust. These Zionist or Nationalist Jews were despised, demonised and exterminated mercilessly by

Western nations, people who were brainwashed into thinking that they were *Lebensunwertes Leben*.

Nowadays, the same forces have convinced those on the extremes of politics, left and right, that the Jews are bad. There is a new wave of anti-Semitism that is growing, just as the left is promoting a puritanical agenda. Reaction formation was behind the evangelical fervour of the progressive movement and the Eugenics movement it gave birth to. Hitler symbolised the final destination of such an evil creed, one that exterminated millions of Jews.

Yet, what many may not realise is that 'anti-Semitism' also exists amongst jews. Those who are ashamed of their Jewish heritage, those who are afraid of being targeted themselves, are those who have adopted reaction formation. For what Churchill called 'Bolshevic Jews'[116] are the enemy of the traditional Jew. The Kapos were Jews who collaborated with the Nazis to keep their fellow jews in line in the concentration camps. They were said to be vicious, some more vicious than the German guards themselves. They were afflicted with the same anxiety and guilt. Yet, inflicted with the hatred born of reaction formation, they did the opposite of stick together. They despised and condemned their fellow prisoners for being what they were – Jewish. The question of what it means to be anti-Jewish

---

[116] (Winston Churchill, 1920)

is often disguised by a person saying that they are anti-Zionist, without having an in-depth knowledge of Jewish history and tradition. This really means that they are pro-Palestinian, who they view as the 'victims', and part of their intersectional alliance Without sufficient knowledge in P$_2$ and free thought in A$_2$, the crowds simply chant their support for the 'Palestinians' and disavow their own anti-Semitic impulses.

Eric Berne may himself have suffered from reaction formation since he changed his family name from Bernstein to Berne. My own family may have done the same since I was once told that 'Green' was often chosen as a surname by Jews who feared persecution or adverse reaction from gentiles.

Reaction formation is what is behind many of the moral crusades we see today. The anti-fascist is fixated on seeing fascism around him, yet he dares not imagine that this is but an illusion. For the feeling of hatred he experiences is born of the anxiety and guilt that lies within him, yet he dare not look at that. Without a P$_2$, he has forgotten wise lines like "Let anyone among you who is without sin be the first to throw a stone…,"[117] from the Bible. Or, from Confucius, 'If you look into your own heart, and you find nothing wrong there, what is there to worry about? What is there to fear?'

---

[117] (John, 7:53-8:11)

Reaction Formation is often what lies behind the hateful rhetoric of those who profess to love, those who worship an ideal of humanity, instead of liking people for being people.

President Trump is either loved or hated, like marmite... but the intensity of hatred has led to this being called 'Trump Derangement Syndrome'[118]. This hatred is so intense that I believe it may be a case of reaction formation. A good friend of mine, a fellow therapist, commented on what Dickens called "the attraction of repulsion."[119] He said, "It has always seemed to me, for example, that the left is actually attracted to Trump, whilst professing to be repelled. i.e. They LOVE to HATE, so much that they cannot resist him. Interesting that they never do this with truly dangerous fascists. Hence my thesis that the Left of the purist variety always ends up colluding with fascism."[120]

---

[118] (Charles Krauthammer/Jonah Goldberg, 2015)
[119] (Efraim Sicher, 2007)
[120] (Author anonymous, 2020)

Healing the split

Is it possible to heal the split? Many years ago, I would have said yes, nowadays I am less optimistic. Why?
I have broken up many playground fights when I was a school teacher in the 1980s. Each time, I would remove the protagonists from the crowd that had gathered; a crowd that would be egging on one person or the other. The crowd would be playing the role of the Inciter (a form of Persecutor), in the game of 'Let's you and him fight'. I would follow up on my intervention by speaking to each party individually, getting their point of view and then speaking to them together, me acting as a mediator. Most of the time, the issues that had led to the fight were resolved, as each person engaged their A_2 and P_2 to balance out their rage in their C_2. This fight I would call a divide or disagreement, but not a split.

In a split, each person loses their individual identity. They are no longer two individuals fighting it out, but two representatives, one of each rival group; so, they are fighting on behalf of the clique they belong to. Like two rival gangs or tribes. Their fierce belonging needs have overtaken all their individual needs. I would not be able to get the two fighters to see sense and give up on the fight. They would be unwilling to access A_2 or P_2. Even if they pretended to stop, their gangs would continue the fight, selecting different fighters if necessary.

What changed the fight into a split? It is down to group dynamics. In some groups, people are allowed to retain their individuality. They can act under their personal agency and still retain membership in the group. However, in some groups, there are rigid requirements to becoming a group member. One of those requirements is that personal agency and individualism are given up. Cults and gangs are renowned for this, as the group tenets demand a surrendering of personal beliefs, attitudes and individual preferences to those of the group. Hence, Groupthink is based on this concept.

Ideological psycho-political groups use the same group dynamics as found in cults and gangs. That is, the 'individual' is a concept that they will not countenance. This process is one of eliminating individualism and imposing collectivism. Political Progressive John R. Commons, is recorded as saying that "social progress required the individual to be controlled, liberated, and expanded by collective action." "Individuals, Ross maintained, were but 'plastic lumps of human dough,' to be formed on the great 'social kneading board.'"[121] Following this, individual needs are reformulated in accordance with the collective. Maslow's

---

[121] (Thomas Leonard, 2016, all quotes)

original Hierarchy of Needs[122] **applies to individuals** but needs to be... Reformulated **for the collective.**

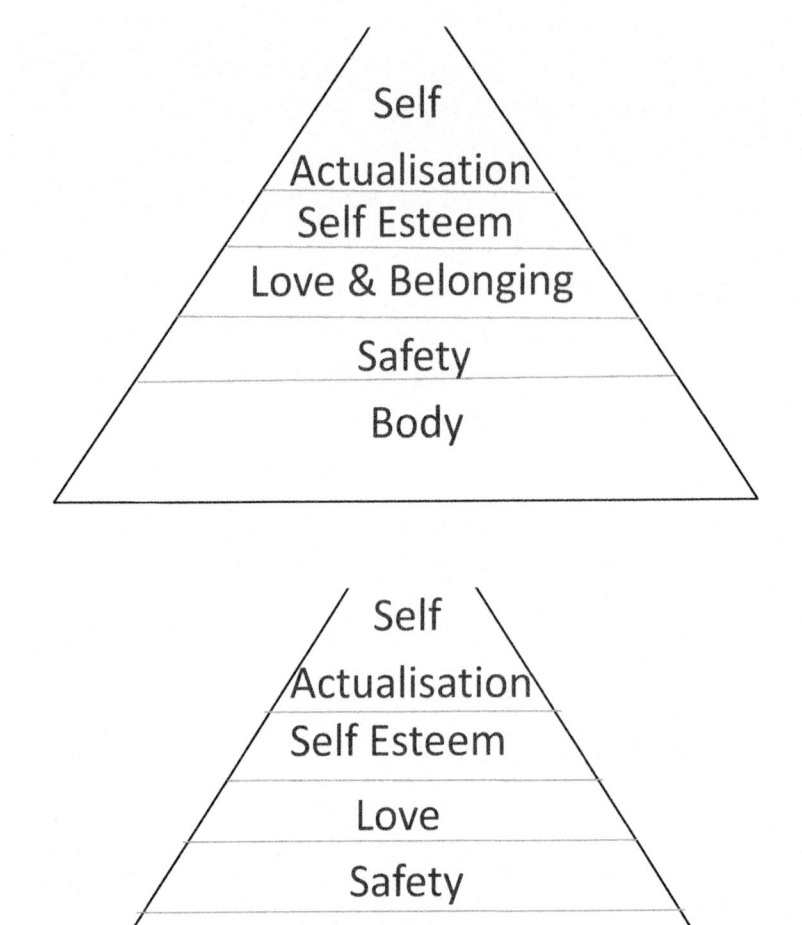

```
         Self
     Actualisation
      Self Esteem
    Love & Belonging
         Safety
          Body
```

```
         Self
     Actualisation
      Self Esteem
          Love
         Safety
          Body
        Belonging
```

[122] (Abraham Maslow, 1943)

'Belonging' has become the most important need, even more important than body or safety needs. The desperate need to belong (conform) is the glue that binds every individual to the demands of the gang, the cult and the totalitarian state. Projective identification is the force that brainwashes group members into compliance with 'Groupthink'. It is the antithesis of free, individualised thinking.

So, the reason for splitting can often be laid at the door of 'adapting' as a way of 'belonging'. Groups that demand that the primary allegiance of their members is to the group, rather than to their friends or family, are really religious cults; even if the religion involves the worship of the Guru or ideology, rather than a supernatural God. We might call them cliques, for this close-knit group does not readily allow others to join them. Personal agency together with the needs of the individual, first have to be surrendered to the will of the group. This is different from a person signing up to a therapy group, where the person knows what the group demands are in advance and they have made an A_2 choice. This then is the true price of belonging at all costs... that we do not consider or reconsider the cost of continuing to belong to the rival 'cliques' that now exist in society. It explains the nature of the split world we inhabit. Moreover, we have not arrived at this by natural means. We continue to allow ourselves to be psychologically and politically

265

manipulated into a tribal standoff, and possibly worse. A split is divided tribal loyalty.

Thus, a split refuses to heal, since the hatred of the 'other side' is collectivised, and is not an individual one. The 'other' is then not seen as a person, but as a demon representing all that is bad. This split is what I experienced at the Live 8 concert in 2005 - when the crowd mass, suddenly and collectively, hated the 'English' - a prejudice took hold of the crowd and all individual expression was extinguished. In that instant, the Kumbaya moment was lost.

The same dynamics are present when a couple fall out and their 'family' and 'friends' take sides, supporting one against the other. The Family & Friends bias and prejudice feeds C_2 but does nothing to encourage A_2 or P_2. P_1 becomes the dominant force and is not open to the sanity that the excluded A_2 and P_2 could bring to bear. That is why people who have joined a cult refuse to listen to wisdom or common sense. It takes something like a 'collectivised' intervention to counteract the brainwashing they have received... and they are unlikely to ask for that help themselves; many of us are uncomfortable in imposing an intervention, as it goes against our belief in personal agency and individual freedom.

In the past, I have used the following question to try to access the personal agency and some A$_2$: "Would you rather be right or be in a relationship?" Most individuals, when presented with the stark reality of losing their friend, would snap out of seeing red, and see sense instead. Nowadays, since people are less individuated and more a spokesperson for their own 'gang', the real answer is usually, "to be right, of course"; even if each pretends to answer that they value the relationship. The two parties may appear to agree on a reconciliation, yet it may well not hold the moment they report back to their base group. The need to belong to their partisan group is often greater than their friendships, their spouses, their children or any relationship that threatens to oust them from their own 'cult'. Their tribal loyalty kicks in.

Many celebrity couples nowadays, often break up in the public domain. The most recent case is that of Johnny Depp and Amber Heard. Their differences are externalised, and the media encourages the public to take sides. "Do you support him or her?" Without realising it, this is once again a binary choice, which is no choice at all. It serves to turn the divide into a split, where the couple is made part of Group A or Group B. As their personal differences are tribalised, they are guaranteed never to resolve their differences and it becomes something akin to a blood sport.

Splits are particularly arduous on anyone who attempts to resolve them. If the person who wants to help is a 'Rescuer', they usually, in the end, get turned on by both parties; each now blaming the helper rather than each other for the original split. In TA we refer to this as the game of 'IWOTTH' or 'I was only trying to help'. The naïve Rescuer usually ends up becoming the 'Victim'. Alternatively, if the person attempting to fix the split is mischievous, they will be coming from a 'Persecutor' position and may turn a split into a disaster, ensuring that no future reconciliation can take place. Mainstream Media and Social Media are experts in turning such a crisis into a drama.

In short, 'splitting' reveals an agenda that wishes to abolish the 'individual' and make us all into parts of a 'collective'. Why then is this so significant? Because, the USA and the UK have a history of Freedom predicated on 'individual freedom', not on 'collective freedom'. These two countries led the call for the abolition of slavery in the 1800s. 'Collective Freedom' on the other hand is freedom for no one, and could also be viewed as akin to 'slavery'. Totalitarianism is the final destination for the collective version of freedom.

Many now view Isaiah Berlin as warning us of this peril, in his article on 'Two Concepts of Liberty'[123] and his book 'Freedom and its betrayal: six enemies of Human Liberty'.[124]

"But to manipulate men, to propel them towards goals which you – the social reformer – see, but they may not, is to deny their human essence, to treat them as objects without wills of their own, and therefore to degrade them. That is why to lie to men, or to deceive them, that is, to use them as means for my, not their own, independently conceived ends, even if it is for their own benefit, is, in effect, to treat them as subhuman, to behave as if their ends are less ultimate and sacred than my own. In the name of what can I ever be justified in forcing men to do what they have not willed or consented to? Only in the name of some value higher than themselves."[125]

---

[123] (Isaiah Berlin, 1958)
[124] (Isaiah Berlin, 2002)
[125] (Isaiah Berlin, 1958)

How we got to here – a summary:

1. From a moral perspective, some people have been persuaded that they ought to be 'better people'. This has led to a movement that has a religious quality to it: PURITANISM.
2. This campaign is unlike that of the Civil Rights movement that pushed for rights for everyone. This movement wants more rights for some while denying rights to others.
3. Postmodernism redefines the nature of Reality, from one based on Objective FACTS to one based on Subjective PERCEPTIONS. i.e. 'All Truths are subjective'.
4. Likewise, THOUGHT based on Reason, Evidence and Logic has been replaced by THOUGHT that is based on the Imaginal, Intuition and Sentiment.
5. Also, Knowledge or epistemology is challenged by revisionist history and relativistic values. Words have become redefined to alter their meaning, so become useless as a means of arriving at a common point of reference.
6. Common sense is nowadays neither common nor does it make sense.
7. With the notion that "the personal is political," feminists removed the sanctity of private thoughts and feelings, thereby allowing politics to infiltrate everything.

8. In Postmodernism, the TA terms, A_2 and P_2 no longer exist. All reality is based on P_1, A_1 and C_1, all of which make up C_2.
9. The effect of the above is that more and more people have become 'narcissistic' or self-centred and self-absorbed.
10. Postmodernists made these changes to cover up the collapse of socialism in the 20th century. Their 'felt sense' that socialism was good and true, trumped the facts and logic argument that evidenced the contrary. This denial is central to postmodernism and this 'felt' version of reality underpins the whole postmodern movement.
11. Groupthink is where people in groups surrender their personal beliefs and adopt those of the group. It is akin to hypnosis or mass hysteria.
12. Political activists, like Saul Alinsky, exploited Groupthink and other psychological techniques to pursue their political agenda. A group is easier to manipulate psychologically than a free-thinking individual.
13. **Postmodernism has birthed an illiberal humanist movement, one that uses authoritarian means to hold onto power.** It aims to destroy individualism and all values arising from modernism. The destruction of liberty is called Liberticide.
14. The political left has formed an intersectional coalition (the enemy of my enemy is my friend), made up of

disparate groups. These groups try to set aside their individual agendas in favour of a 'common agenda'. Some of these agendas are dangerously extreme political ideologies.

15. The intersectional or WOKE alliance includes many Marxist activists. They believe that humanity is collective and finds true expression in groups.

16. There is now a split in society between those identifying as WOKE and those who are AWAKE. **WOKE identify their problems, not as ones that originate within themselves, but ones that are caused by the unjust world they see around them.** AWAKE believe in personal agency and decry 'victim culture'. They identify as 'Traditionalists' or 'Classic Liberals,' preferring Dr Martin Luther King Jr's definition to that of Malcolm X.

17. The TA definitions of 'Victim' and 'Rescuer' have been redefined as 'victim' and 'rescuer'. **In TA the Victim is defined as the person who views himself as one down, deserving to be mistreated or unable to get by without help.** The postmodernist 'victim' is anyone who asserts that they are such, and usually gets status points in so doing. **The TA 'Rescuer' steals the personal agency from the Victim.** The postmodern 'rescuer' is usually seen as right-minded and is called a Social Justice Warrior, 'SJW'.

18. In postmodernism, **the whole concept of First Order Ego States becomes redundant.**

19. Projective Identification is a brainwashing technique, where one person can force their will into another; as developed in cults and gangs.
20. We inhabit a 'split world'. A 'psychological split' is an inability to simultaneously hold opposing thoughts, feelings or beliefs. A person who 'splits' sees the world in terms of black or white – all or nothing. They cannot talk across opposing narratives.
21. Political activists benefit from keeping us 'split'. I list, several 'Jedi Mind Tricks' that enable them to do so.
22. Human Nature is at the heart of political disagreement amongst AWAKE and WOKE. Is man a sentient organism with a free will, or is man a mechanistic being, who can be externally reprogrammed? Is there any divinity therefore in man or are we no more than a product of biological evolution?
23. Is the West losing its liberal and democratic values and becoming more like Communist China? Are we losing our Individualism and personal freedoms?
24. Is the plutocracy using the Covid-19 crisis to install itself as a totalitarian world regime, under the Green agenda and Woke ideology? The Great Reset plan sets this out.
25. In TA psychotherapy, an A_2 is vital. Before any meaningful work can begin, the therapist and client need to establish a baseline as to what constitutes Reality. This is called DECONTAMINATION. Without this, Traditional TA becomes meaningless.

26. Ego State profile diagrams show how the personality structure has changed since the time of Eric Berne. The world of the Child has been given more weighting than that of the Adult.
27. In a split world, Empathy is not always the solution, it can be the problem. This is ultimately a form of narcissism that passes as caring.
28. Empathic immersion is a dangerous form of manipulation, as used by Big Tech.
29. Reaction Formation is the 'reformed smoker syndrome'. It leads to puritanism and an 'urge to purge' - repent or perish!
30. The 'desperate' need to belong to certain cliques, has become the most important need in Maslow's traditional 'Hierarchy of Needs' pyramid.
31. Postmodernism aims to defeat Individualism and impose Collectivism.
32. Postmodernism aims to eliminate Negative Freedom (which resulted in the abolition of slavery) and install Positive Freedom (which leads to the re-establishment of slavery via the Totalitarian state). Isaiah Berlin warned us of this danger.

The Gimmick and the Switch

Before I conclude, I wish to explore a couple of concepts from TA. The first arises from Berne's Game theory: The Game formula: Con + Gimmick = Response, Switch, Cross Up, Payoff.

He considered that this formula was found in all psychological games. He described the first move as the 'Con'. That is a superficially plausible assertion, that carries with it a hidden or ulterior message. This could be "I'm a vegan now" which carries the ulterior 'I'm a better person for changing my eating habits... what about you, are you a 'better' person too?'

The Con only works on someone who carries an insecurity. This could be a shame about their nation being racist in the past (i.e. USA), or a world-dominating empire (i.e. UK) or a nation that started a World War (i.e. Germany). This is what is called an 'original sin' by Roman Catholics. It is, a personally felt 'badness' for the professed 'sins' of our ancestors. This leads to a shame or fundamental insecurity about ourselves, and a fear of being called out as 'bad'.

The insecure person (Gimmick), falls for the bait and in the above example, becomes defensive in response to the assertive Con. Becoming defensive could appear as an angry rebellion or as adaptive compliance with the Con. Whatever their response, they feel guilty or ashamed of their past and must either defend it or decry it. They are in the game.

The Response part will therefore appear as either an angry disavowal or as compliant appeasement. Either is a sign that both players are in a game. At the Switch, the real self makes a momentary appearance. The person who was angry, yet who may have secretly harboured shame at the fact that they too believed they were 'bad,' will suddenly acquiesce and become tearful and sorry for their sins. They have suddenly declared their sin and are at the mercy of the SJWs. However, as many then discover, there is no redemption narrative, so no way of ever feeling sorry enough to satisfy some on the social media circuit.

The person who initially responded with adaptive compliance may have really felt angry at being called out. Yet, their passivity prevented them from saying anything. Now, as the 'Vegan' continues to push their point - their moral superiority - the recipient becomes angrier and angrier. Eventually, they explode and call out their friend/partner over their professed moral superiority. This switches their roles and game dynamics. It is at this point friends or partners fall out. They now clearly belong to very different groups.

The switch is the emotional change point, like switching rail tracks. Switches indicate that emotional charges have built up; it is the discharge of these intense charges that result in everyone feeling confused (Cross Up), misunderstood and wanting to blame the other (Payoff). In modern times, we have allowed ourselves to become convinced that there are only two tribes we can belong to, so the differences are often irreconcilable. This too is a con for it is putting our need to be in the right camp, ahead of our human need for friendship and tolerance of difference.

The Functional Model of Ego States Revisited

In the 1960s many TA therapists would see clients born before the 1950s. Functionally these clients had an excess of Controlling Parent and Adapted Child. Therapists saw the need to develop their clients' Nurturing Parent and Free Child. In that way, they would arrive at a more balanced personality. The hidden bias amongst many TA therapists was to see no fault in NP or FC. Whereas CP and AC were considered constrictive parts of the personality and therefore 'bad', NP and FC were seen as liberating and therefore 'good'. Controlling Parent was even called 'Critical Parent' by many who did not see its positive attributes.

However, as clients born in the 1960s and after came into therapy, many therapists may not have appreciated that the world had changed. So, to continue promoting NP and FC would have unintended consequences - their clients would end up with a Narcissistic personality structure instead of a balanced one. CP and AC represent for me the Justice side of the equation, whereas NP and FC represent Love. By overemphasising Love and downplaying Justice, the Functional model becomes unbalanced. Too much love, too little justice.

Narcissists have an inconsiderate, self-centred and self-satisfying character, oblivious to the actual needs of others and adopting somewhat aloof and 'superior' stances on life. Their child-like nature is carefree and attractive yet they are often unreliable and have too little consideration or sympathy for the real plight of others. Often, they compensate for this lack by adopting 'feel-good' stances on humanitarian projects rather than concentrating on being real in real relationships. This False Self persona protects them from experiencing their Real Self which they really struggle with. In real up-close relationships, the intimacy becomes too much for them to handle so they prefer to busy themselves with projects and distant causes.

According to Stephen Johnson[126], narcissism has two splits. Most narcissists operating in their False Self do not come into therapy. They are usually attractive, seductive and vivacious or can be plain and hidden, yet hold an I+U-or 'superior' view of themselves. Only when their False Self fails do they come looking for help. By then, they are in the grips of their Symptomatic Self and have lost the sparkling look, are often depressed and full of self-loathing. They have decompensated. What many do not realise is that bad as things may appear, there is still another split lying in wait. Most narcissists do not ever get to this point since they simply use therapy as a springboard to get themselves back

---

[126] (Stephen M Johnson, 1987)

to their 'absolutely fabulous' selves. They get what they want to hear and use therapy to get their feel-good strokes.

Some narcissists do visit their second split and come to their Real Self. However, they often react with such a visceral hostility to this part of themselves that they are horrified by what they experience. They see what they've been trying so hard to not be. This is where they need a real loving Nurturing Parent and not the over-indulgent Nurturing Parent that they've introjected. Being able to love this REAL part of themselves is what real therapy ought to be about, not just getting strokes for the False Self. It is 'tough love' that they need.

Zoe came into therapy believing that she made poor choices when it came to men. She said she was attracted to 'bad boys' yet they always let her down. She had tried dating those she didn't feel as drawn to, but they always turned out to be boring and couldn't keep her interested. She owned up to being promiscuous and had a roving eye. She enjoyed sex but it usually ended badly when either she or her partner had affairs. Zoe was passionate about her 'save the whales' activist work, wanted children and longed for a more 'normal' life.

Zoe had both a strong NP and FC, yet little Adult and a weak CP and AC. Her previous therapists were 'kind' and 'nice' but she didn't feel they really understood her. They had indulged her by pandering to her wants and letting her 'be herself'. Clearly, this had not been what Zoe needed, as she already had too many permissions yet few boundaries. I assessed Zoe as having a narcissistic personality, needing to value not just herself but to see others as subjects just like her. She needed to build her options in A, be more aware of her boundaries around others CP, and learn to take things more slowly in relationships AC. Also, she needed to work out her value system, since some of her values contradicted her other values.

Zoe came into therapy in 1994. She was a popular member of my therapy group, yet was seen as somewhat naïve and immature. The other group members stroked her for keeping to her boundaries, especially around anti-social men who sometimes hit on her. She went back to a boyfriend with who she regretted breaking up and made the relationship work. She eventually decided against having children but did take on a job in a special school as a teaching assistant. This she felt enabled her to feel useful as a mother figure without overwhelming her. Zoe was able to heal the narcissistic splits in her personality and the therapy was deemed successful

Someone with a similar personality style to Zoe came into therapy in 2015. Amy had similar issues but the world had changed since 1994. Amy became very popular in the group, especially amongst the male members. Amy was attractive and vivacious, much as Zoe had been. However, the group became split when it came to Amy. Some would take her side and view her as the Victim of men who tried it on with her. Others would become critical of her poor boundaries and thought she had only herself to blame. The split group was not a therapeutic experience as it only served to exacerbate the narcissistic splits already present in Amy. The therapy was not successful and I had to supplement it with several individual sessions which eventually replaced the group sessions.

Earlier, in Part One of this book, I described my experience with groups since 2010. It was the rising number of individuals with narcissistic splits that made the groups untenable. These narcissistic individuals were child-like, naïve and gullible. However, unlike children, narcissists assume a morally superior stance and worldview that is held together by denial. They will not accept negative feedback nor will they self-reflect. They are hyper-critical of others who adopt a different attitude to them.

The Narcissism Epidemic

This then is the world we now live in. So many of us in the West have narcissistic personalities, that it has been referred to as a 'Narcissism Epidemic',[127] where the alarming rise of narcissism has had catastrophic effects at every level of society. Even the world economy has been damaged by risky, unrealistic overconfidence. This is the world of the naïve and gullible, those most easily manipulated and exploited by sociopathic and psychopathic elites.

When I started seeing private clients in 1992, some had splits in their personalities and were referred to as Borderline Personality Disorder (BPD). They were usually self-destructive, and as Masterson[128] had noted, "I have such a poor self-image and so little confidence in myself that I can't decide what I want, and when I do decide, I have even more difficulty doing it." These chaotic individuals were considered difficult to work with, had Jekyll and Hyde personalities, and over the next 25 years occupied up to 10% of my practice.

Other clients also had personality splits but were more composed, often were high achievers and again as Masterson noted, "I was denied promotion to chief

---

[127] (Jean M Twenge & W Keith Campbell, 2010)
[128] (James Masterson, 1981)

executive by my board of directors, although my work was good, because they felt I had poor relations with my employees. When I complained to my wife, she agreed with the board, saying my relations with her and the children were equally bad. I don't understand. I know I'm more competent than all these people." These were individuals with Narcissistic Personality Disorder (NPD). They were grandiose, had a child-like seduction and a 'Be Perfect' compulsion. They were operating almost exclusively in their Child ego state, since they were trapped in denial, did not self-reflect, lacked proper self-other perspective, had impaired reality testing and maintained a grandiose sense of themselves where they would not accept negative feedback from others. About 5% of my clients had this diagnosis in 1992; by 2018 I was seeing more than 50% who fitted this category. This was the Narcissism Epidemic.

Although several authors such as Freud[129], Kernberg[130] and Masterson had written about the Narcissistic personality style, it was Heinz Kohut and Stephen Johnson who became my go-to authors. Kohut thought of it as a developmentally-arrested individual, someone who had failed to individuate at an early age, who lacked sufficient parental mirroring and who relied on a False-self persona. In particular, it was

---

[129] (Sigmund Freud, 1914)
[130] (Otto Kernberg, 1975)

Kohut's capture of the narcissistic rage that caught my attention:

"Human aggression is most dangerous when it is attached to the two great absolutarian psychological constellations: the grandiose self and the archaic omnipotent object. And the most gruesome human destructiveness is encountered, not in the form of wild, regressive, and primitive behaviour, but in the form of orderly and organized activities in which the perpetrators' destructiveness is alloyed with absolute conviction about their greatness and with their devotion to archaic omnipotent figures."[131] He then goes on to say, "I could support this thesis by quoting Himmler's self-pityingly boastful and idolatrous speeches to those cadres of the SS who were executors of the extermination policies of the Nazis."

This narcissistic rage is what I had seen in crowds that turned into violent mobs. It is what resulted in the Blackshirts, the Brownshirts, the Klu Klux Klan and more recently in Antifa and BLM riots. They were acting "...with absolute conviction about their greatness and with their devotion to archaic omnipotent figures." That is, with a moral superiority based on devotion to an unbending guru, ideology or religion. This is Groupthink in action.

In 2020 we are witness to a Woke movement that is based on narcissism and its allied rage. In cults and religious movements, people are kept in C_2 without access to A_2 or P_2. In that way, they become compliant puppets that serve

---

[131] (Heinz Kohut, 1972)

their masters. Intelligent-yet-gullible people are the most likely to get caught up in this spell since they are often the most socially awkward and have the most desperate need to belong and be accepted.

We have all contributed to the creation of this narcissistic society. It has been fed by a mixture of greed, materialism and consumerism which has tempted many into ignoring the dangers posed by shiny objects. Big business, Big tech and celebrity culture have all led us on a Pied Piper walk to a catastrophic ending. Yet, behind the scenes, those of us who are Awake, see the sociopaths and psychopaths at work, planning, plotting and scheming to thwart our individual freedoms. The plutocracy craves power more than anything else and the narcissist is unable or unwilling to consider that they are being switched off to the real dangers and distracted onto imaginary dangers instead. Through global causes that play on their collective sentiments, they deny their real feelings and march in unison as once did the SS. In their quest to do good, they have become the modern-day puritans, those who seek to purify life and exterminate viewpoints other than their own. Kohut was right to warn us of the narcissistic compulsion - an absolute conviction and devotion to their human God. It has become a perverted version of what Humanism once stood for – Hubris... for humans are not God!

Viktor Frankl[132] once confronted Abraham Maslow, about "...his 'hierarchy of needs,' who said that once basic needs (food, shelter) are met, then the intangibles such as love, meaning, and self-actualization can be fulfilled. But Frankl disagreed. He told Maslow how people did not have their 'basic' needs met in the concentration camps, but it was the 'higher' needs (i.e., meanings, love, and values) that proved to be much more relevant to their chance of survival. Maslow revised his ideas and said, "Frankl is right." Frankl emphasized that it's not about 'having what you need to live' but asking yourself, 'What am I living for?' The most affluent societies have all their basic needs met, but they lack something to live for, and neurotic disorders tend to increase."

---

[132] (Viktor Frankl as told by his grandchildren, 2017)

The way forward

Where will all this end?

Splits in society have a history of ending badly. Either in genocide, apartheid or civil war to mention a few. A split is different from a divide since there is no middle ground to hold the two extremes. As neither side looks to give way anytime soon, we are living in anxious times.

On Freedom

Two opposing visions of Freedom separate the sides. The negative version sees people as fundamentally free to do what the law permits. Yet, it sees these laws as necessary to constrain the worst excesses of human behaviour; a behaviour it judges as a mixture of good and bad. The USA constitution expresses this view, and as Thomas Sowell[133] says, it arose from the constrained vision of human nature. Its roots are in the belief that people are neither fundamentally good nor fundamentally bad. It recognises that some people are vulnerable, yet also that they have Agency. It seeks to promote equality of opportunity not equality of outcome. Proponents see the alternative view as one that promotes 'dependency' on state handouts, rather than promoting 'independence'. Negative freedom encourages a strong work ethic, a stable nuclear family,

---

[133] (Thomas Sowell, 2007)

individuated thinking through education, religious freedom and the nation as a unit of pride and integration... **Teach a man to fish!**

Those who prefer the positive version of Freedom, view it as something that some people need help in accessing. That, Freedom is not automatically accessible to all. Thus, they promote the welfare state, government intervention and affirmative action for those they judge as needy. They want equality of outcome... **Give a man a fish!** The Humanistic philosopher Erich Fromm, from the Frankfurt School, wrote 'The Fear of Freedom' in 1941.[134] He argued strongly for positive freedom and that man's freedom needs to move from the negative to the positive. For Fromm, positive freedom marks the beginning of humanity as a species conscious of its own existence free from base instinct. Fromm believed in 'freedom to' change society, but he also believed in 'freedom from' internal prohibitions such as guilt and conscience. He saw these as repressive instead of counterbalancing man's natural egocentricity. His hopeful take involves human beings evolving beyond their instinctual aspects, which characterise lower animal forms. His hope is what still propels many to this day.

---

[134] (Erich Fromm, 1941)

On Human Evolution

Fromm hoped that all people would become self-regulating. I too would like that dream to be true. It is a wonderful dream, but it is a pipe-dream - because it is based on a belief in human nature that people are fundamentally good. Yet, this is contradicted by the fact that so many resist the call and continue to hate others, sometimes in the name of love. For what is freedom for some, is slavery for others. This will always be the case, for there is more than one side to any debate. Just as there is no such thing as 'settled science' since science is not a status quo. The idea that we become 'better people' is all a question of definition. Do we mean more considerate of those less fortunate than ourselves? Do we mean more obedient, or less spontaneous? Or less obedient and more spontaneous? Who decides? How do we avoid the collisions that will occur when each person does exactly as they please? Have we abandoned the 'golden rule' for 'mob rule'?

There is a vast difference between the notion of the 'natural' evolution of people and 'engineered' change. Some, like Erich Fromm, Saul Alinsky and those promoting positive freedom, have abandoned Karl Marx's contention that capitalism will naturally evolve into socialism, once the workers revolt[135]. They have sought instead to help it along, through social engineering and manipulating the populace 'by any means necessary'. This is what is causing the split in society. The failure of socialism has driven some to desperate measures to force the change through. They have done this by using psychological coercion and ensorcellment spells such as Projective Identification, fostering an attitude of 'moral superiority' such as Reaction Formation, and by the promotion of Empathy as a wise, 'sentimental good'. They have pushed through a 'divide and conquer' narrative that now threatens social cohesion and our future as a peace-loving people. Did Erich Fromm believe that people would have to be forced to become 'self-regulating', or is that an oxymoron?

On Biology

Yet, there is one biological fact that has been ignored, something known by those who specialise in dog breeding and producing new hybrid plant varieties. The simple fact is, that once a forced change is left alone in nature, the changes revert back to their original types. The same can be said of humans. That is, a person must want to change their script. It cannot be imposed on them to do so. Otherwise, a person can change their behaviours

---

[135] (Karl Marx, 1850)

temporarily, but will revert to old behaviours once time passes. For the underlying structural attitudes will not have really changed, because the person did not decide it for themselves. Without personal agency, an extrinsic motivation will not hold. Rewards and punishment may help facilitate change, but they will not be enough to stabilise it.

On Will

TA works with individual agency, not with a collective will. For instance, I cannot work with a client who has been brought along to therapy by a loved one such as a partner, in the hope that I can perform some form of voodoo magic on them. Nor can I transform the attitude of a prisoner, simply because the prison service deems it necessary. In other words, unless the client wants to change and is prepared to do the necessary hard work, the therapy has no chance of working. Behaviours may change, but not the deeper attitudes. Personal agency is vital for both changes to happen and for those changes to remain stable once the therapy stops. As long as an individual realises for themselves that they wish to change, there is hope that this change will be permanent. To do so, they need to be presented with viable alternatives from which to choose. Otherwise, they have not really made a choice. Instead, the choice has been made for them and has therefore been imposed. An imposed choice will eventually be rejected, no matter how wonderful other people think it is. Once the individual stops getting the positive strokes for having become a 'great person', the real person is left to deal with who they have allowed themselves to become... and that may no longer be so pretty.

On the Dialectic

What would Hegel make of all this? The future of people in the West is looking very shaky at present. As we enter the new decade, it appears that we are battling postmodernism with resurgent modernism. If the thesis is postmodernism then its antithesis is resurgent modernism, what will the synthesis look like? What many may not realise is that the synthesis or settlement reached is not meant to be final. It simply becomes the new thesis, as there are no 'final solutions'. Is there yet a way of addressing perceived injustices within a common frame of reference that promotes personal agency and rids us of 'victimhood culture'?

On Compromise

There is a need to arrive at common definitions of some words, for we all need to find an accommodation if we are to avoid severe consequences. The idea that 'the pen is mightier than the sword' is best remembered, since force and violence must not be allowed to rule. The power to seek compromise is an Adult quality, a mediation between the Parent and Child ego states.

This is made very difficult, if not impossible when ideologies predominate and each side is only willing to listen to its base. For, since tribal loyalties have been stoked, the passions released are ones that will fight to the death...only, this is now no longer simply a fight **for** the ideology. It has become a fight **against** the imposition from the other side, a side viewed as demonic and evil... where people are being forgotten in a bid to save 'humanity'.

On Equality

I had always thought that equality was a bad idea, and still do - dividing the cake equally regardless of how much effort everyone put into baking it. I had however thought that equity potentially addressed the issue of injustice, giving more to the more deserving. What I see, however, is the reappearance of the age-old question of 'who decides?' In an age of unreason and factless assertion, equity looks even worse than equality - those who shout loudest and threaten us with violence, get the whole cake!

On Morality

I think we can all agree that there is a need for a modern, common definition of personal morality. The left has relied on empathy and Rousseau's pity for its formulation. That places it for me in the field of 'collective sentiment,' rather than in 'private feeling' for another person or living thing. Sentiment is too open to social manipulation such as 'virtue signalling' and SJW judgements, to be at the root of such a personal morality. I much prefer Roger Scruton's formulation of moral philosophy[136] as originating in the subject/object way by which we relate to one another. For example, I see myself as a subject, but may view you as an object, a means to an end. Unless I see you too as a subject, with your own needs, thoughts, feelings and beliefs, I may treat you badly, as if you were an item of mine. It is through this I-Thou exchange that true morality begins to make sense.

On Violence

For, if we really love humanity as so many profess, we need to appreciate it in all its hues and colours, its many shades of opinion, its inspirational as well as disappointing ideas. We must stop playing at God and trying to force the

---

[136] (Roger Scruton, 2017)

unnatural evolution of people. History shows us that it is possible to get people to rise up in support of an ideology. However, it also shows us that it usually leads to another group of people rising up against it. History also tells us that people have been willing to adopt severe means to achieve their ends... even war when it comes to it. People have not changed that much, for all the wishful thinking in the world. When it comes to it, reason usually kicks back in before neighbour will attack neighbour. Peace is what many profess to want, but violence cannot be a means of achieving it. Hitler wanted to bring peace to Europe by subjugating its people and exterminating those he considered inferior. Are we seeing this 'urge to purge' ideology all over again?

On Extremes

As religious puritanism and Marxist political ideology continue to dominate, there may be no settlement. Unless, and until, enough people push back and say no more! It is as well to remember the late Christopher Hitchens, who warned us, "There is also a special *ad hominem* venom on the left, and an extreme willingness to attribute the very lowest motives to those who transgress its codes..."[137]

---

[137] (Christopher Hitchens, 2000)

No good will come of replacing our shared history in P$_2$, with a PC code that is imposed on all humanity. No good will come of repressing dissident thought and not allowing a plurality of ideas in A$_2$... for it will lead to the end of individual freedom, of personality itself and to **"a boot stamping on a human face — forever"**, as per Orwell.[138]

These 'identity' ideologies are not the same as the fight against slavery, where there was a persuasive argument that made sense. Neither is it like the Civil Rights protest of the 1960s, where Dr Martin Luther King Jr's voice rang true. Instead, this is all based on Critical Theory, a deceptive narrative for its aim is to impose the political and cultural ideology of Marxism on the rest of us. If we are all to make it past this point, we must wake up to the bigger picture all around us. Fear and panic are being pumped into people at an unprecedented rate, whether by Climate change predictions, fears of economic collapse or the latest Covid-19 advice. While we are not asking searching questions, the planet is being re-organised economically, politically and socially. Would we wish to wake up tomorrow to a world that we do not recognise? One where totalitarianism had been imposed while we slept? Only by switching on our Adult thinking and Parent wisdom are we going to assert our individualism and get past this point.

---

[138] (George Orwell, 1949)

On Fear

Extreme ideologies have their basis in fear. Whether the fear is that of difference or the unknown or of deeply held prejudices of tribal origins… whatever their origins, fear is still fear. It is fear that morphs into terror if it is allowed to grow into a monstrous version of itself. Because unlike fear, which is a feeling that can be expressed and worked through, terror is something very different. Terror is a physiological, spiritual and panic-inducing escalation of fear. Terror is fear in a set-concrete form. It cannot be worked through, only resisted. For as Carl Jung said:

"It is becoming more and more obvious that it is not starvation, it is not microbes, it is not cancer, but man himself who is his greatest danger: because he has no adequate protection against psychic epidemics, which are infinitely more devastating in their effect than the greatest natural catastrophes"[139].

Once we hit terror, at first anger usually tries to compensate. Anger is our attempt to resist the imposition of another's will. Through engagement and dialogue, we can get heard and hear others whose viewpoints may differ. Anger is a non-violent passion. Faced with another's fear, it

---

[139] (Carl Jung, 1933)

can appeal to reason or common humanity. Faced with terror, anger can resist. However, anger can itself morph into a monstrous form – Rage or Hatred. Hatred is likewise a physiological, spiritual and panic-inducing form of anger. In its set-concrete form, hatred is annihilatory energy, that seeks to destroy. Once hatred takes hold, it can override our common humanity. This is what I believe we are seeing in society today, not in individual form, but in mass collective movements. Movements that believe they are about promoting love… yet are in the business of creating hate. Hate for the 'other'. Just as in religions of old, modern religions are in the business of converting the heathen, the infidel, the unbeliever. Underlying this is their belief in repent or perish! The 'urge to purge' in action.

On Ideology

Based on fear and insecure in the fundamentals of their own belief system, these movements are exporting hatred not love. We need to wake up to that and resist their 'by any means necessary' attitude. This will require courage and conviction on the part of us that believe in personal liberty, the right to think our own independent thoughts and the rule of law that applies equally to everyone. Hatred is not conquered by violence, but by the force of conviction in a common humanity. That we are all created equal, some with particular gifts, some recipients of better nurture, but equal nonetheless. For, there are no better people, but there are worse ideologies. The effects of lapses in nurture can often be healed by free engagement in psychotherapy. These nurture lapses may be a result of family breakdown, abuse, neglect or elusive aetiologies. That is something we can strive for. An Adult recognition that 'blame' is not a viable standpoint, since it denies us our human dignity and keeps us all stuck as child-like beings.

In Conclusion

At the start of this book, I referred to what I learned in Scotland in 2005. I enjoyed my stay in Edinburgh, the friendliness as well as the pride of the Scottish people I met. The Scottish people have a proud history of contributing to scientific achievements, great philosophers, medical breakthroughs, educational reform and other cultural achievements. Additionally, they are great fighters and are renowned for their passion and whiskey! They have a lot to be proud of. Yet, that was not what was first triggered in the crowd in Murrayfield Stadium that night. It was hatred of the English. That was their divisive loyalty triggered, a collectivised hatred of 'the other'. Eddie Izzard managed in time to remind everyone of the Scottish pride IN Scotland and not in defining themselves AGAINST England. The singing of Flower of Scotland brought the crowd back into a pride that was not hatred. I saw first-hand how a less accomplished presenter would have struggled to turn hatred back into pride. He succeeded in reminding them of their unifying loyalty. A unified pride in who they are. A nation that once stood firm against an authoritarian imposition from King Edward II's army in the Battle of Bannockburn in 1314.

Pride born of prejudice is different from informed pride. For pride that comes from wisdom counteracts both guilt and shame. The Gay movement promotes Gay Pride to counteract the prejudice that results in guilt and shame. Likewise, if we are to halt the slide into surrendering our virtues to those who are determined to destroy Western values, we must promote pride. Yet this pride must be informed and not underpinned by prejudice. Pride informed by wisdom is PRIDE IN who we are, rather than HATRED AGAINST who we are not. Informed pride involves re-establishing P_2 or the wisdom of elders. It involves restocking our libraries, uncensoring books, bringing back education to replace indoctrination and finding worth in the experience of an older generation that has actually lived a life. For, without a Parent ego state, all that is left is hypothetical, speculative, assertion, unbridled optimism and a disregard of consequences, dangers and tried-and-tested ideologies that are known to fail. Informed pride resists guilt and shame.

I am not English, yet felt for the plight of 'the other' when the hatred of anything English was triggered in the Murrayfield crowd. Only then did I feel threatened, because I did not belong to the 'in-group'. I was an outsider and lost the protection I had felt up until that point. I sympathised with the plight of 'the Jew' as a symbol of what it must be like to be hated for being different. That this fear, terror, anger, hatred complex, must run so deep in humankind, that it can be, and is still being stoked to this day. This is nothing but prejudice, a belief that has been passed down over the generations. It is a hateful belief because it pits person against person for no reason other than intolerance of difference. We must tolerate people, but not divisive ideologies, especially those that masquerade as 'peace and love' movements – we must strive to become aware of the authoritarian impulses in our P_1 and develop A_2 and P_2. We must raise ourselves from a 3D (P_1, A_1, C_1) to a 5D (P_1, A_1, C_1 A_2, P_2) version of the personality; if we, as people, are to make it past this point in our time on this planet.

Epilogue

In the current lockdown of 2020, we are experiencing the effects of having our liberties curtailed. Instead of finding common ground between those that fear the biological pathogen and those that fear the loss of personal liberty, there is a split; that is, extreme viewpoints are taking hold and little dialogue or debate is happening. As fear takes hold, its effect is to exacerbate the split already present in society. While some welcome the restrictions to personal liberty in an effort to stay safe, others fight for the right to stay free. In the closed system produced by the imposed measures, there is less opportunity for people to meet, interact and for different ideas and opinions to be shared and discussed. In the absence of a space to express, experiment with and receive honest feedback, individuals are susceptible to becoming overwhelmed, vulnerable and to accepting indoctrination. It is reminiscent of the isolating effect of a prison or a cult, where there are restrictions on the normalising effects of healthy human interactions. Without such cross-fertilisation, and a diversity of ideas and opinions, anxiety prevails and many of us are all too susceptible to losing heart. The cost to our mental health has yet to be calculated, yet the invisible cage has already claimed many victims. The effect of confinement, and in many cases solitary confinement, will be too much for many to bear. Doubtless, there will be an increase in anxiety and depressive illnesses as well as suicide.

In the meantime, as the smoke eventually clears, we will emerge to a world that has been re-engineered socially, economically and politically. Aldous Huxley and George Orwell warned us that liberty dies when we voluntarily give up our personal freedoms. In a recent speech by Jonathan Sumption, formerly a Supreme Court Justice, he too warns us of this danger. Entitled "This is how freedom dies: The folly of Britain's coercive Covid strategy",[140] he sets out his concerns. This is a plea for reason and common sense to replace fear and panic. Will his plea for reason be enough to wake us up to the dangers of over-reacting with panic? Perhaps we will come together as one people, or perhaps this is truly the dawning of the authoritarian 'Age of Aquarius'?

The World Economic Forum appears to be behind a lot of what has happened in 2020. It is interesting how quickly it has formulated a plan to reshape the world under the title 'Covid-19: The Great Reset'[141]. Using the Covid-19 pandemic as its trigger, it begs the question: just how long was this plan in the making? This plan was not suddenly put together in 2020. It, therefore, leads to another question:

---

[140] (Jonathan Sumption, 2020)
[141] (Klaus Schwab & Thierry Malleret, 2020)

was this virus an accident or was it unleashed upon an unsuspecting world? That is the question few are asking in the Mainstream Media. China appears to have escaped with little scrutiny from the West, suggesting that it was complicit with the Great Reset plan.

The plan makes chilling reading. It envisions a totalitarian world, shaped by the plutocracy, where we voluntarily give up our individual freedoms so that we feel 'Happy'. It is a world dominated by big corporations and slave people who continue to believe their lies. Their propaganda reminds me once again of the Puritan method for recruiting religious followers:

In short: first, produce the problem and then offer a cure that is worse than the problem itself. Desperation born of panic will result in many surrendering their liberties, but not all people will succumb to that. What happens to those who refuse to take the vaccine or those who peer behind the curtain and see the plutocracy at work?

2008 was the year when the plutocracy crashed the Western economy. 2016 saw the rise in Populism with Brexit in the UK and the election of Donald Trump in the USA. Ordinary people had woken up and broken their programming. They disobeyed their 'rulers'. Both events shocked the plutocracy and their quest for a global empire. Since then, they have sought both to deny the people their voice and their vote. Is the WEF a group of benevolent world leaders or a criminal cabal that is in charge of our planet? Years ago, this sounded like a conspiracy theory, nowadays less so.

The threat we face is from fear itself. Fear, if left unchecked, leads to panic, then desperation and a willingness to submit to illiberal practices - all in the name of certainty, safety and public interest. It is the weapon of tyrants, those that wish to mobilise the crowd and turn citizen against citizen. Intellect alone is not enough to stand up against panic. The one thing that works is the absence of fear, what is called potency. The absence of fear is what grownups marshal when they bring calm to a young child suffering from panic such as night terrors. If the parent shows no fear and remains calm, the child will slowly begin to calm down.

In the UK, many people have been put to sleep and silenced by covid, by BLM, by a complicit press, by a police force that sides with lawbreakers and arrests those that believe in the law, by politicians who have either been bought or threatened. Fear prevents people from rising up against this authoritarian religion. The answer must lie in resistance and not in violence, otherwise, we will end up destroying all that we hold dear. There have been many people who have demonstrated peacefully, some of whom have been arrested and fined. They are showing an attitude of no fear. Maligned by the press, they are appealing to people's conscience and therein lies the weakness of the left. This is the same weakness that led to the UK giving up India to Gandhi's peaceful protest and in Martin Luther King Jr's 'I have a dream' speech defeating long-held racist attitudes. Good people eventually saw sense.

The left fears it is losing, so in desperation, is resorting to violence and to imposing a misconceived plan under the guise of Covid-19. No longer does the left believe that it can use persuasion alone to convert more people to its woke ideology. It fears people rallying around a fearless champion such as a Gandhi or MLK. These fearless champions do exist and those arrested show the rest of us that there is a resistance. To win this fight, we must once again become fearless and a champion will emerge from our ranks. History tells us that. It also tells us that "You can fool some of the people all of the time, and all of the people some of the time, but you can not fool all of the people all of the time." This is a time to muster the courage to fight fear and wisdom to fight ignorance and resolve to fight tyranny.

In the face of an anticipated massacre at Dunkirk, before the evacuation, Churchill turned for solace to the words of George Borrow's 'Prayer for England' written in Gibraltar: "Fear not the result, for either shall thy end be a majestic and an enviable one, or God shall perpetuate thy reign upon the waters."[142] Privately, Churchill was afraid of the burden of responsibility he carried. Yet, Churchill did not let his fear get the better of him. Instead, he provided the nation with the resolve and leadership that it needed and saw the many stranded troops home, inspiring brave souls to sail to France in a flotilla of little ships to save their fellow countrymen. We all need to reconnect with that resolve and fearlessness to stand up for that which we believe in.

---

[142] (John Lukacs, 1999)

References:

1. Christopher Dobson, *The Ponte Vecchio: The old bridge of Florence*, Via Airali 1, 2015
2. Trevor Phillips, *The March of Woke-ism is an all-pervasive new oppression*, The Times, 6th November 2020,
3. Lord Scarman, *The Scarman Report*, HM Home Office, 1981
4. Otto L Shaw, *Youth in Crisis: A Radical Approach to Delinquency*, Hart Publishing Company, 1966
5. Alexander Sutherland Neill, *Summerhill: A Radical Approach to Child Rearing*, Hart Publishing Company, 1960
6. William Golding, *Lord of the Flies*, Faber & Faber, 1954
7. Jonathan Croall, *Neill of Summerhill: The Permanent Rebel*, Pantheon Books, 1983
8. Erich Fromm, *The Fear of Freedom*, Routledge, 1941
9. Otto L Shaw, *Prisons of the Mind*, George Allen & Unwin Ltd, 1969
10. Miguel de Cervantes Saavedra, *The Ingenious Gentleman Don Quixote of La Mancha*, Francisco de Robles, 1605 & 1615
11. Barbara Ann Brennan, *Light Emerging*, Bantam Books Inc., 1993
12. Erik Erikson, *Childhood and Society*, Image Publishing Company, 1951
13. Ian Stewart & Vann Joines, *TA Today: A New Introduction to Transactional Analysis*, Lifespace Publishing, 1987
14. Donald W Winnicott, *The Child, the Family and the Outside World*, Pelican Books, 1964

15. Carl Jung, *Psychological Types or The Psychology of Individuation*, Kegan Paul Trench Trubner, 1921
16. Eric Berne, *Transactional Analysis in Psychotherapy: A Systematic Individual & Social Psychiatry*, Grove Press Inc, 1961
17. Thierry Bokanowski & Sergio Lewkowicz, *On Freud's "Splitting of the Ego in the Process of Defence"*, Karnac Books, 2009
18. Barbara Somers, *The Fires of Alchemy: A Transpersonal Viewpoint*, Archive Publishing, 2004
19. Paul Vitz, *Psychology as Religion: The Cult of Self-Worship*, The Paternoster Press, 1977
20. Sigmund Freud, *Civilisation and its Discontents*, Penguin, 2004 (First published 1930)
21. William Butler Yeats, *The Second Coming*, The Dial, 1920
22. Thomas Moore, *Care of the Soul: A Guide for Cultivating Depth and Sacredness in Everyday Life*, Harper Collins, 1992
23. Jean Illsley Clarke & Connie Dawson, *Growing Up Again: Parenting Ourselves, Parenting our Children*, Hazelden, 1989
24. Martin Luther King Jr, *A Testament of Hope: The Essential Writing of Martin Luther King*, Harper Collins, 1991
25. Malcolm X & Alex Haley, *The Autobiography of Malcolm X*, Ballantine Books, 1987
26. Richard Delgado et al, *Critical Race Theory: An Introduction*, NYU Press, 2017
27. Yuval Harari, *Sapiens,* Harper Collins USA, 2015
28. Christopher Booker, *Groupthink: A study in Self Delusion*, Bloomsbury Continuum, 2020

29. Francis Bremer, *Puritanism: A Very Short Introduction*, Oxford University Press, 2009
30. Friedrich Hayek, *The Road to Serfdom*, Routledge, 1944
31. Joel Kotkin, *The Coming of Neo-Feudalism: A warning to the Global Middle Class*, Encounter Books, 2020
32. Isaiah Berlin, *Two concepts of Liberty*, Clarendon Press Oxford, 1958
33. Georg Wilhelm Friedrich Hegel, *The Phenomenology of Spirit*, Notre Dame Press, 2019 (First published 1807)
34. Karl Marx & Friedrich Engels, *The Communist Manifesto*, London, 1848
35. Friedrich Nietzsche, *Thus Spoke Zarathustra*, Ernst Schmeitzner, 1882-1893
36. Friedrich Nietzsche, *The Birth of Tragedy and the Genealogy of Morals*, Anchor Books, 1956 (First published 1887)
37. Martin Heidegger, *Being And Time*, SCM Press, 1962 (First published 1927)
38. Abraham Mansbach, *Heidegger's Critique of Cartesianism*, Contemporary Philosophy, 6 1998
39. Immanuel Kant, *Critique of Pure Reason*, Aegitas 2016 (First published 1781)
40. Todd May, *Between Genealogy and Epistemology: Psychology, Politics and Knowledge in the thought of Michel Foucault,* Penn State University Press, 1993
41. Henri de Lubac, *The Drama of Atheist Humanism*, Ignatius, 1944
42. Paul Vitz, *Psychology as Religion: The Cult of Self-Worship*, Wm B Eerdmans Publishing Co, 1977
43. Philip Larkin, *This be the Verse*, New Humanist, August 1971

44. Antonio Gramsci, *Prison Notebooks: Volumes 1, 2 & 3*, Columbia University Press, 2011
45. Martin Jay, *The Dialectical Imagination: A History of the Frankfurt School and the Institute of Social Research, 1923 – 1950*, University of California Press, 1996
46. Theodor Adorno & Max Horkheimer, *Dialectic of Enlightenment*, Allen Lane, 1973
47. Adolf Hitler, *Mein Kampf*, Ford Edition, 2010 (originally published 1925)
48. Ian Davidson, *The French Revolution: From Enlightenment to Tyranny*, Profile Books, 2016
49. Saul Alinsky, *Rules for Radicals*, Vintage Books, 1989
50. Irving Janis, *Groupthink*, Houghton Mifflin, 1982
51. Karl Popper. *The Logic of Scientific Discovery*, Routledge, 1958
52. Thomas Kuhn, *The Structure of Scientific Revolutions*, University of Chicago Press, 1962
53. Gregory Wrightstone, *Inconvenient Facts: The Science That Al Gore doesn't want you to know*, Silver Crown Productions LLC, 2017
54. Dr Patrick Moore, *Fake Invisible Catastrophes and Threats of Doom*, Ecosense Environmental, 2021
55. Rex Fleming, *False Alarm: The Rise and Fall of the Carbon Dioxide Theory of Climate Change*, History Publishing Co LLC, 2020
56. The Times Newspaper, *The Times view on Harry Miller, Twitter and the trans debate: Thought Police,* February 15th 2020
57. Yuval Harari, *Sapiens,* Harper Collins USA, 2015

58. Evelyn Beatrice Hall, *The Friends of Voltaire*, GP Putnam's Sons, 1906
59. Richard Blackwell, *Behind the scenes at Galileo's Trial*, University of Notre Dame Press, 2008
60. Carol Swain, *The New White Nationalism in America: Its Challenge to Integration*, Cambridge University Press, 2002
61. Thomas Sowell, *Intellectuals and Race,* Basic Books, 2013 and *Discrimination & Disparities,* Basic Books, 2019
62. Gustav Mueller, *The Hegel Legend of 'Thesis-Antithesis-Synthesis*, Journal of the History of Ideas, 19(3): 411–14. 1958
63. Thomas C. Leonard, *Illiberal Reformers: Race, Eugenics and American Economics in the Progressive Era,* Princeton University Press, 2016
64. Ibid
65. Jean Jacques Rousseau, *The Social Contract,* Everyman, 1993 (originally published 1762)
66. Fanita English, *Sleepy, Spunky and Spooky,* Transactional Analysis Journal 2:2 April 1972
67. Erik Midelfort, *A History of Madness in Sixteenth-Century Germany,* Stanford University Press, 2000
68. Teddy Amenabar, *What students mean by terms like 'safe space',* The Washington Post, 19th May 2016
69. Sarah Fiarman, *'Unconscious bias: when good intentions aren't enough,* Educational Leadership, November 2016, <u>74</u> 3
70. Jordan Peterson, *12 rules for life; an antidote to chaos,* Allen Lane, 2018
71. Hanna Segal, *Introduction to the work of Melanie Klein,* New York Basic Books, 1974

72. Ronald David Laing, *Self and Others*, Penguin, 1969
73. James Grotstein, *Splitting and Projective Identification*, Jason Aronson Inc, 1981
74. Ibid
75. Dave Rubin, *Don't Burn This Book: Thinking for Yourself in an Age of Unreason*, Constable, 2020
76. James Grotstein, *Splitting and Projective Identification*, Jason Aronson Inc, 1981
77. Josh Halliday & Heather Stewart, *BAME MPs accuse Priti Patel of gaslighting in racism debate*, The Guardian Newspaper, 11th June 2020
78. Matt Ridley, *Nature Via Nurture: Genes, Experience and what makes us Human*, Harper Perennial, 2004
79. Roger Scruton, *On Human Nature*, Princeton University Press, 2017
80. Thomas Hobbes, *Leviathan*, Simon & Schuster, 1651
81. Jean-Jacques Rousseau, *A Discourse on Inequality*, Penguin classics, 1984 (originally published 1754)
82. Martin Heidegger, *Being and Time*, Harper Perennial, 2008 (originally published 1927)
83. Jean-Paul Sartre, *Existentialism is a Humanism*, Methuen & Co, 1948
84. David Berlinski, *Human Nature*, Discovery Institute Press, 2019
85. Steven Pinker, *Enlightenment Now: The Case for Reason, Science, Humanism, and Progress*, Allen Lane, 2018
86. Mark Bray, *Antifa: The Antifascist Handbook*, Melville House, 2017
87. Donald Carveth, *The Still, Small Voice*, Karnac Books Ltd, 2013

88. Larry Arnn, *Churchill's Trial: Winston Churchill and the Salvation of Free Government*, Thomas Nelson, 2015
89. Thomas Sowell, *A conflict of Visions: Ideological Origins of Political Struggles*, Basic Books, 2007
90. Colin Wolin, *The Politics of Being: The Political Thought of Martin Heidegger*, Columbia University Press, 2016
91. Stephen Hicks, *Explaining Postmodernism: Skepticism and Socialism from Rousseau to Foucault*, Ockham's Razor, 2013
92. Isaiah Berlin, *Two Concepts of Liberty*, Clarendon Press Oxford, 1958
93. Jean-Jacques Rousseau, *The Social Contract*, Wordsworth Editions, 1998 (originally published 1762)
94. Francis Fukuyama, *The End of History and the Last Man*, Free Press, 1992
95. Klaus Schwab & Thierry Malleret, *Covid-19: The Great Reset*, Forum Publishing, 2020
96. Rupert Darwall, *Green Tyranny: Exposing the Totalitarian Roots of the Climate Industrial Complex*, Encounter Books, 2019
97. Douglas Murray, *The Madness of Crowds; Gender, Race and Identity*, Bloomsbury Continuum, 2019
98. Donald Carveth, *The Still, Small Voice*, Karnac Books Ltd, 2013
99. Ibid
100. Heinz Kohut, *The Analysis of the Self: A Systematic Approach to the Psychoanalytic Treatment of Narcissistic Personality Disorder*, International Universities Press, 1971
101. Robert Berezin, *Empathy is a False God*, Psychology Today, 8th June 2015

102. Paul Bloom, *Against Empathy: The Case for Rational Compassion*, Vintage, 2018
103. James David Vance, *Hillbilly Elegy: A Memoir of a Family and Culture in Crisis*, William Collins, 2016
104. Robert Berezin, *Empathy is a False God*, Psychology Today, 8th June 2015
105. Paul Bloom, *Against Empathy; The Case for Rational Compassion,* Vintage. 2018
106. Christopher Booker, *Global Warming: A case study in Groupthink: How science can shed new light on the most important 'non-debate' of our time*, The Global Warming Policy Foundation, 2018
107. Donald Carveth, *The Still, Small Voice*, Karnac Books Ltd, 2018
108. Robert Berezin, *Empathy is a False God*, Psychology Today, 8th June 2015
109. Simon Parkin, *Has Dopamine got us Hooked on Tech?* The Observer (Technology), 4th March 2018
110. Fernanda Herrera et al, *Building Long-Term Empathy*, Plos One, 17th October 2017
111. Jorge Herrero et al, *An Immersive Virtual Reality Educational Intervention on People with Autistic Spectrum Disorders (ASD) for the Development of Communication Skills and Problem Solving*, Educ Inf Technol, 18th November 2019
112. William Shakespeare, *Hamlet*, 1601
113. Carl Binding & Alfred Hoche, *Allowing the Destruction of Life Unworthy of Life: Its Measure and Form*, Suzeteo Enterprises, 2012

114. A N Wilson, *Charles Darwin: Victorian Mythmaker*, John Murray, 2017
115. Shelby Steele, *White Guilt: How Blacks and Whites together destroyed the Promise of the Civil Rights Era*, Harper Perennial, 2007
116. Winston Churchill, *Zionism versus Bolshevism: A Struggle for the Soul of the Jewish People*, Daily Herald Newspaper, February 8th 1920
117. John, 7:51 – 8:11
118. Esther Goldberg, *Trump Derangement Syndrome*, American Spectator, August 2015
119. Efraim Sicher, *The Attraction of Repulsion*, Brill/Rodopi, 2007
120. Author Anon
121. Thomas C Leonard, *Illiberal Reformers*, Princeton University Press, 2016
122. Abraham Maslow, *A Theory of Motivation*, Psychological Review, 1943
123. Isaiah Berlin, *Two Concepts of Liberty*, Clarendon Press Oxford, 1958,
124. Isaiah Berlin, *Freedom and its Betrayal: Six Enemies of Human Liberty*, Chatto & Windus, 2002
125. Isaiah Berlin, *Two Concepts of Liberty*, Clarendon Press Oxford, 1958
126. Stephen M Johnson, *Humanising the Narcissistic Style*, WW Norton & Co,1987
127. Jean M Twenge & W Keith Campbell, *The Narcissism Epidemic: Living in an Age of Entitlement*, Atria Books, 2010

128. James Masterson, *The Narcissistic and Borderline Disorders*, New York: Brunner/Mazel, 1981
129. Sigmund Freud, *On Narcissism: An Introduction*, Read Books Ltd, 2013 (originally published 1914)
130. Otto Kernberg, *Borderline Conditions and Pathological Narcissism*, New York: Jason Aronson, 1975
131. Heinz Kohut, *Thoughts on Narcissism and Narcissistic Rage*, Psychoanalytic Study of the Child 27: 360-400, 1972
132. Fran Grace, *Viktor Frankl and the Search for Meaning: A conversation with Alexander Vesely and Mary Cimiluca*, Parabola 42 No1, Spring 2017
133. Thomas Sowell, *A Conflict of Visions*, Basic Books, 2007
134. Erich Fromm, *The Fear of Freedom*, Routledge, 1941
135. Karl Marx & Friedrich Engels, *The German Ideology*, Martino Fine Books, 1850
136. Roger Scruton, *On Human Nature*, Princeton University Press, 2017
137. Christopher Hitchens, *Unacknowledged Legislation Writers in the Public Sphere,* Verso, 2000
138. George Orwell, *1984 Nineteen Eighty-Four*, Secker & Warburg, 1949
139. Carl J Jung, *Modern Man in Search of a Soul*, Routledge Classic, 2001 (originally published 1933)
140. Jonathan Sumption, *This is how Freedom Dies: The Folly of Britain's Coercive Covid Strategy,* The Spectator, 28th October 2020
141. Klaus Schwab & Thierry Malleret, *Covid-19: The Great Reset*, Forum Publishing, 2020
142. John Lukacs, *Five Days in London; May 1940*, Yale University Press, 1999

Printed in Great Britain
by Amazon